BUNRAKU

BUNRAKU

The Art of the Japanese Puppet Theatre

DONALD KEENE

photographs by
KANEKO HIROSHI, 1933 –   illus.

講談社

KODANSHA INTERNATIONAL LTD.

Distributed in the United States by Harper & Row, Pub-
lishers, New York; in Continental Europe by Boxerbooks,
Inc., Zurich; in Canada by Fitzhenry & Whiteside Limited,
Ontario; and in the Far East by Japan Publications Trading
Co., P.O. Box 5030 Tokyo International, Tokyo. Published
by Kodansha International Ltd., 2-12-21, Otowa, Bunkyo-ku,
Tokyo 112, Japan and Kodansha International/USA, Ltd.,
599 College Avenue, Palo Alto, California 94306. Copyright
in Japan, 1965, by Kodansha International Ltd. All rights
reserved. Printed in Japan.
                              LCC 65–19187
                       ISBN 0–87011–193–0
                     JBC 3074–783763–2361
Hardback edition, 1965
Revised paperback edition, 1973

The text
is dedicated to
CAROLYN KIZER

CONTENTS

INTRODUCTION

PUPPET and marionette shows have intrigued me since I was a child and saw my first *Aladdin and his Wonderful Lamp*. Something uncanny, and at the same time enormously endearing, gave these shows an allure which in later years I was mistakenly to attribute to the guilelessness of extreme youth. The association of puppet shows with the schoolroom proved so strong, indeed, that once I considered myself beyond the stage of childish pleasures I felt rather ashamed of my lingering fondness for the make-believe world of little wooden people. Only much later was I to discover, after beginning the study of Japanese, that in one country at least the puppet theatre had developed not only as an adult entertainment, but as the vehicle of a magnificent dramatic art. I came to realize that Bunraku (the common name for the Japanese puppet theatre) occupies a most important place in Japanese literary and theatrical history alike, and by no means belongs to the frivolous class of entertainments associated with puppets and marionettes in other parts of the world. I learned too that Japan's greatest tragic dramatist, Chikamatsu Monzaemon, wrote not for actors but for the Bunraku puppets, and when I later had the chance to attend the Bunraku Theatre, I found that the audience today as in the past is there to enjoy a true dramatic performance rather than an amusing display of the dexterity of the operators. I noted how much more frequently one saw an old lady brush away the tears induced by some pathetic scene than one heard the sounds of laughter we might expect in the West at Punch and Judy shows.

My active interest in Bunraku began long before I was able to visit Japan and witness a performance. In 1949 I completed a doctoral thesis about one of Chikamatsu's plays, depending on descriptions, photographs, and my imagination when attempting to describe its effectiveness as a work for the theatre. Much as I tried to persuade myself that a dramatic illusion could be sustained, despite the presence of three men operating each of the puppets in full view of the audience, the photographs did little to reassure me. The first thing to strike my eyes, whichever photograph I examined, was the face of the principal operator, then his costume, and only thirdly the doll in his hands. How, I wondered privately, could one forget the operators when they seemed so much more alive than the puppets?

Nevertheless, when finally I had the opportunity to see Bunraku in Japan, I discovered that the claims of enthusiasts had not been mistaken; after the first few minutes of uncertainty I found myself being drawn into the world of the puppets, and if I looked at the operators' faces afterwards it was by deliberate choice, and not because they drew attention to themselves. I remember particularly from my first experience of Bunraku the energetic exit of one puppet, dragging the three operators after him. The photographs, I could only conclude, had lied; their record of Bunraku performances did not correspond to reality.

What was my amazement, then, when last year I saw Kaneko Hiroshi's Bunraku photographs! For the first time, I felt, the magical life of the puppets onstage had been captured, and I understood why. The audience requires time once a Bunraku play begins to forget the presence of the

9

operators, but photographs provide no interval for the process of moving from the human beings to the world of the puppets. Mr. Kaneko, perceiving this, and noticing also that at times in each performance the operators are concealed from the audience's sight by the movements of the puppets, waited for these moments to take his pictures. The puppets, freed of human ties, reveal in his photographs the peculiarly tragic beauty we sense in witnessing an actual performance.

The present book originated in a sensitive artist's recreation in photographs of the evanescent illusions of a Bunraku performance. For my part, I have added historical and interpretative material, in the hopes of increasing the reader's appreciation of this extraordinary art. Here too, the illustrative photographs of Mr. Kaneko have been essential. I have devoted my attention chiefly to Bunraku as a theatrical, rather than as a literary, art. Readers interested in the texts are respectfully referred to my book of translations *Major Plays of Chikamatsu* and to other works listed in the bibliography.

One further word, on the subject of the name Bunraku. Strictly speaking, it designates exclusively the puppet theatre in Osaka descended from the one founded by Uemura Bunrakken (or, Bunraku-ken) some 150 years ago. I have used it, however, to describe many varieties of puppet entertainments in Japan, including independent regional traditions and even the early puppet theatre, before the advent of Bunrakken, who gave his name to the art. Purists may object, I know, but the alternative would have been to call what is essentially the same art by a number of different names. Bunraku, incidentally, is not pronounced in normal English fashion, but as if written something like *boon-rah-koo*. Although derived, as I have said, from a man's name, the characters for Bunraku 文楽 have a meaning too, "the pleasure of literature," not an inappropriate designation for a theatre where the texts have always been treated with extraordinary deference.

DONALD KEENE

[NOTE : Throughout this book, Japanese names appear in the Japanese order, with family name first and given or adopted name last.—EDITOR]

BUNRAKU

I. THE PLEASURES OF BUNRAKU

MAN HAS been making images of himself for so many millennia and in so many parts of the world that this habit has come to seem an instinctive part of human behavior. Whether the compulsion expresses itself in the form of cave paintings or manuscript illustrations, monumental sculptures or miniature dolls, it has proved irresistible, and has led to the creation of many supreme triumphs of art. But, not content with fashioning semblances of himself, man has sought also to impart to them life and movement like his own. The clockwork man which strikes the hours, the doll which cries "Mama!" when tilted forward, the puppet which obeys the will of an unseen hand, all testify to man's delight in creating imitations of himself. In every instance the creator hopes that his imitation will convince by fidelity to its model, and that it will be accorded the highest compliment a mechanical doll, a puppet or a marionette can evoke—the exclamation, "It seems to be alive!"

The oldest known puppets, those of ancient Egypt, were probably used in religious ceremonies to represent the actions of the gods, perhaps out of some belief that human imitation of the gods would be sacrilegious. Eventually, however, puppet shows ceased to be ritual performances and became instead popular entertainments, especially farces, as we know from the familiar spectacle of Punch and Judy banging logs over each other's head with the exaggerated vigor possible in a theatre which need not take human weaknesses into consideration. Indeed, the possibility of representing non-human actions—whether flying through the air or splitting in two—remains an indispensable part of the charms of puppets, and although an operator, depending on his skill, may convince us that the puppet performing at his instigation is really alive, it is essential that we realize with a part of our mind that the puppet is not human, but moves in a world of its own. The pleasure we take in puppets is similar to that of watching the antics of monkeys. We see in them our own familiar gestures, exaggerated in their "human" quality by our awareness that non-humans are performing them. Monkeys have not sufficient intelligence to sustain our interest in their actions, much less to cast them into an artistic pattern, but the puppet, though lacking life of its own, can borrow life from its operator, and become whatever he desires. It can be a god or a stammering idiot, but never itself, for it has no identity. It is equally suitable for sacred rituals or the crudest of farces.

Obviously, the more skilled an operator and the more advanced the mechanism of his puppet or marionette, the more convincing will be the illusion that a living creature is performing. If the operator is a master, his puppet can seem the very embodiment of the words of the play; the puppet is unlike an actor, who always retains something of his own personality, regardless of the role. But the puppet forfeits its claim on our attention if it is not imbued with the mystery of the non-human being magically possessed of human attributes. It is conceivable that a marvelously talented operator could manipulate a doll of human proportions so adroitly that an audience would be incapable of distinguishing the doll from a human being. Such excessive realism, as Chikamatsu Monzaemon noted, far from pleasing the audience, would probably disgust instead; Chikamatsu insisted that stylization in art and not literal fidelity is what the audience craves. A puppet which was indistinguishable from a human being would certainly not be his equal, for it would lack intelligence and individuality. The danger of over-realism is present today in exceptionally skillful varieties of marionette shows, where, after our initial astonishment at the realism of the movements, we are likely to grow bored with the expressionless little creatures so uninspiringly performing as Faust, Tamino, or the Queen of Denmark.

Stylization must be present not only in the manipulation of the puppets but in the texts they perform. It is possible, of course, to put puppets through the motions of *Faust*, *The Magic Flute*, or even *Hamlet*, but in these parts they are at a grave disadvantage, for they cannot achieve the individual coloring of an actor, nor do the texts permit them to display their superhuman capabilities. It is better to see a puppet performance of *Aladdin* than of *Hamlet*, for *Aladdin* at least has room for fantasy. Miracles, prodigies of speed, sudden transformations, and defiance of the law of gravity or the weight of numbers are all easily within the puppets' abilities, but they cannot sit still for long. In the West this has meant that plays written specifically for puppets have generally been intended as fast-moving entertainment for children, but in Japan stylization has been achieved without loss of literary excellence.

Bunraku is the one theatre of dolls for which literary masterpieces have been especially composed. Its techniques have been much improved since its inception in the sixteenth century, but unlike similar shows in the West, it was never, even at the crudest, considered a theatre primarily for the young and foolish. Its progress, resulting from a steadily increased awareness of dramatic possibilities, may be measured in terms of the additional demands made on its audiences, as well as by the more usual standards of improvement in the texts, the puppets, and the music. Each step in the direction of further realism has generally been accompanied by a simultaneous step in the direction of non-realism, as if those responsible for the fate of Bunraku knew of the dangers of surfeiting the public appetite for verisimilitude. Originally (as in some regional theatres today) the puppet operators supplied necessary bits of dialogue, but when more literary texts were adopted it became essential to employ a chanter to declaim the lines. At first he remained hidden behind the scenery, but precisely when the texts became more realistic and closer to the circumstances of ordinary life, the chanter was moved from backstage to a place before the audience, as if to deny the illusion that the puppets were speaking for themselves, and to insist on the primacy of the written word. The texts in turn were written in an often non-realistic idiom in order to provide maximum opportunities for the puppets to reveal their unique capacities. The audience today divides its attention variously between the chanter and the samisen player, the puppets and the operators, and yet somehow it is able to surmount these seeming distractions and impediments to a unified impression, the results of a non-realistic style, and to experience instead the satisfaction of complete entertainment.

The demands of realism and non-realism might be expressed instead as demands of drama and aesthetics. To achieve more powerful dramatic effects the Japanese invented puppet heads with movable eyes, mouths, eyebrows and, in some special instances, noses and ears, but to satisfy the aesthetic conviction that a small head was more attractive than a large one, the puppet heads, no matter how advanced in construction, continued to be disproportionately small. The audience accepted this convention in the interests of beauty. Similarly, the female puppets, though provided with hands of great flexibility and delicacy, normally have no feet because it was felt that the lines of the kimono (which reaches to the ground) are more beautiful when uninterrupted by feet. On the other hand, the left arm of the puppets is very much longer than the right one, not because of aesthetic principles, but because the three-man puppet (an invention intended to afford greater realism and dramatic expression) requires the operator of the left arm to stand farther away from the puppet's body than the operator of the right arm. The audience accepts this convention too, or may not even notice the difference in the lengths of the arms, for it never expects literal accuracy of details. Bunraku, at any rate, is immune to the temptation known in certain theatres of the West of trying to persuade the audience it is watching reality and not a play.

The stylization of Bunraku extends to the language of the texts. Most of the plays in the current repertory date from the eighteenth century, and it is not surprising that the language should be hard to understand today. (Japanese has changed vastly more than English during the same period.) However, even when first composed, passages in the text, particularly the descriptions of the journeys of the suicidally bent lovers or the reflective comments which often open an act, must have been beyond the comprehension of most in the audience. Far from objecting to this elaborate, artificial language, however, the audience accepted it as part of the aesthetic setting of the play. Even the dialogue, which on occasion could be bitingly harsh, is written throughout in a stage language probably never encountered outside the theatre. Attempts in recent years to employ the modern colloquial usually seem ludicrous, because the excessive realism violates the sense of distance necessary in a theatre as delicately poised between reality and non-reality as Bunraku.

Part of our pleasure in watching Bunraku today comes from an awareness, however imprecise, that every gesture by the puppets, every shift in inflection of the chanter's voice, every intensification of accent in the samisen accompaniment is the product of conscious efforts over many years to achieve a perfect balance between realism and non-realism. It is said to take a chanter eight years to master the art of weeping, whether as a girl disappointed in love or as a fierce warrior moved to tears by overpowering grief; but the chanter's protracted sobs and incoherent gasps are scarcely imitative of human expressions of sorrow. They are instead an extraction and exaggeration of the essential qualities of the weeping characteristic of different kinds of people. Hearing the terrible, sustained anguish of the brave man who finally yields to desolation at the loss of his son, we understand more about him than realistic representation would permit. Indeed, as Chikamatsu stated, if a woman in a play were closely modeled on real women, she might conceal her emotions completely, but such accuracy of portrayal would destroy the dramatic appeal of the play. Art, he insisted, lay in the narrow area between realism and fiction.

The stylization of gestures and our continual awareness that we are witnessing a play make it possible for us to accept in Bunraku scenes which would be unspeakably horrible if realistically represented. When Matsuōmaru in "The Village School" examines the severed head of his son, the scene (approached in Shakespeare only by the cruder parts of *Titus Andronicus*) would either fill the audience with terror or stir uneasy laughter if it were not acted with ritual formality. The puppeteers not only make it possible for us to witness this scene without acute discomfort, but by daring to present such extremes of human feeling they may touch levels of emotion deeper than those of more realistic dramas. Performances of the same play by Kabuki actors achieve similar results because the actors continue to observe the puppet traditions. On a more elementary plane, scenes of mayhem or brutality can be funny (in the manner of Punch and Judy) or gruesome (as in the Bunraku play "Summer Festival") without offending our sensibilities.

To visit the Bunraku Theatre today is to witness the re-enactment of many traditions. In comparison, our performances of Shakespeare tend to insist on the contemporary validity of the texts and to deny the centuries separating Shakespeare and ourselves; the actors often deliberately speak the lines of great poetry as if they were prose, and the greatest ingenuity is devoted to inventing new stage business which will not violate the letter of the text. These methods certainly reap more successful financial rewards than the conservatism of Bunraku, but they threaten constantly to falsify, if not destroy, the play as originally conceived. Bunraku has thus far escaped this danger, probably because the conservative (in the literal sense) traditions are so strong in Japan. To cite one example: Customers entering the Bunraku Theatre are likely to buy programs; if not, they can always learn which plays are to be offered and the names of the performers by consulting prominently displayed billboards. Nevertheless, at the beginning of each scene, even as the chanter and his accompanist make their appearance to the right on a revolving platform which swings them into view of the audience, a man dressed in black with a black hood over his head proclaims the start of the play by beating wooden clappers and reciting in sing-song intonation the names of the artists. His presence, strictly speaking, is no more necessary than at a performance of ballet or of Kabuki, where changes of performers from scene to scene are noted in the programs but not reported aloud, yet without this man's announcement Bunraku would seem deprived of an important ingredient. He tells us that we are about to enter a special domain of make-believe, of theatre, and his fading voice as he turns to leave with a final *"Tōzai!"* ("Hear ye!") is the proper signal for the first notes of the samisen.

The chanter generally begins his recitation with a melancholy series of virtually inarticulate sounds. If one examines the text, one will discover that the opening words are often something like "Thus it happened," and are, in fact, the conclusion of the previous scene, which is not performed. A Bunraku program today normally comprises selected scenes from four or five different plays, rather than one entire work, but for musical reasons a performance may thus begin with the dying notes of an earlier act.

Soon after the chanter enters his description of the new scene, the curtain is drawn aside to reveal the set, a naturalistic rendering of a landscape or interior. If the backdrop represents an outdoor scene, it is painted on a series of vertical panels which may be moved laterally to suggest that the characters (who remain in one place) are traveling. If an interior, the gate, framework of the house, and generally one room are depicted, with the suggestion of other rooms beyond. A garden and nearby buildings may also be represented. A doorway at the rear-center of the stage is usual, for it permits the female characters to make spectacular exits, displaying their figures from behind. Very few props are used; unless necessary to the action, the furnishings are generally painted on the backdrop, to allow the operators maximum freedom of movement.

The Bunraku stage, traditionally 36 feet wide, 25 feet deep, and 15 feet high, is divided into various playing areas. The main stage occupies about half the total area, and often serves as the interior of a house. Three raised partitions of different heights run across the width of the stage, standing before the trench-like passages in which the operators work. The partitions conceal the lower half of the principal operator's body, more of the operator of the left hand (who does not wear high-platformed clogs), and almost all of the operator of the feet; at the same time, they provide the apparent floor or ground level on which the puppets walk or sit. To the audience's right is a dais projecting into the auditorium from the stage. There the chanter perches on bulky cushions before an elaborately fashioned reading-stand; to his left, the samisen player sits on a single cushion, dwarfed by the chanter.

By the time the audience has taken in the scene, the first puppet will have made his entrance from the left, often with spectacularly vigorous strides, arms and legs thrust forward as if in excess of energy. Such exaggeration may withhold attention from the three men operating each of the puppets, but soon we will notice and perhaps be distracted by the principal operator, who usually wears a brightly colored, stiffly starched jacket over his kimono, and by his two assistants, less conspicuously attired in black. It takes time to forget their presence, but it regularly happens, as many visitors to Bunraku have discovered, including Arnold Toynbee, who wrote:

In looking on at a Japanese puppet show at Osaka one afternoon in November, 1929, I duly found, as I had been assured beforehand I should find, it possible to entertain the illusion that the puppets were animated by an autonomous life of their own, although the human artists manipulating them were in full view of the spectators. An artistic effect which, in the West, would have been produced by the artifice of keeping the manipulators out of sight, was produced in Japan by their artistry in keeping themselves out of mind notwithstanding their visibility. The Japanese manipulators achieved this *tour de force* of managing to deflect the spectators' attention away from themselves and on to their puppets by making their own movements appear lifeless and their own countenances impassive. They succeeded, in fact, in subjectively effacing their objectively visible living human forms. . .*

Once we have accustomed ourselves to the operators and even forgotten them, we are able to admire the wonderful expressiveness of the puppets and to understand why Japanese audiences accept the awkwardness of three grown men manipulating a doll two-thirds human size. Students of Bunraku invariably insist on the importance of the three men "breathing together"; it can readily be imagined what a blow would be dealt dramatic illusion if the puppet's left hand failed to meet the right hand when a gesture of clapping was intended. The performers at the Bunraku Theatre are of course far beyond the level of such elementary disasters, but clearly they are not all equally accomplished. It is exciting even to watch the least skilled among them, but when a master like Kiritake Monjūrō or the late Yoshida Bungorō manipulates a puppet we sense immediately the presence of life. The flutter of agitation in a woman's breast, the emotion she reveals only in the unconscious movement of a hand, the exquisite moment when, about to make her departure, she hesitates and casts a final glance at the room—all reveal a skill possessed by few real women of communicating to an audience the mysteries of the feminine heart.

If the three operators of a puppet must "breathe" as a single entity, it is no less essential that the three component parts of Bunraku, the narration, the music, and the puppets, "breathe" as one. The music of Bunraku on the whole is not especially tuneful (it is hard to imagine anyone whistling a favorite passage), nor, considering how frequently music from one play was borrowed in composing another, can it be said to be very distinctive. Yet the music is indispensable, both to the chanter, whose voice follows the musical line, and to the operators, who take their signals from the notes of the samisen. The samisen players, though the least feted of the Bunraku artists, bear the chief responsibility for guiding the performance. In a company of the excellence of the Bunraku Theatre the perfect fusion of the three elements seems so effortless as to be almost automatic, but, as a visit to any amateur performance would quickly demonstrate, the apparent effortlessness is the product of many years of individual training as well as of constant rehearsals to improve the coordination of the parts. The samisen player has been called the "wife" of the chanter; his function is not to call attention to his own dexterity but to heighten the effect of the chanter's delivery. It takes about five years, one samisen player estimated, before the partnership of chanter and player "breathes together." The relationship between puppet operators and the samisen is not as close, for they do not function as partners, but an unexpected tempo from the samisen unnerves an operator as easily as a chanter.

The pleasure of seeing these three forms of art combined together is that of a "universal work of art" (or *gesamtkunstwerk*, to use Wagner's term), a performance which satisfies simultaneously by the literary interest of the text, the musical appeal of the samisen, and the visual brilliance of the puppets. In opera, where these three elements take different forms, the music clearly is supreme, and a failure to become deeply absorbed in the story of *Lohengrin* or to be impressed by the stage appearance of the tenor is only a minor disappointment if the music is splendidly sung. In Kabuki, a theatre of virtuoso actors, even a foolish story like *Shibaraku*, which can boast no remarkable musical embellishment, maintains its popularity on the stage because it provides an actor with a magnificent opportunity to display his authority. In Bunraku, the three elements are nearly of equal importance, and a performance by masters of each art provides a thoroughly satisfying theatrical experience.

Of course, as might be said of any complex, traditional art, the connoisseur's enjoyment of Bunraku requires preparation. Unless one understands the text, it is impossible to appreciate fully

* Arnold Toynbee, *A Study of History* (London: Oxford University Press, under the auspices of the Royal Institute of International Affairs)

the skill of the narrator in rendering the emotions behind each phrase, however much one admires the extraordinary vividity of his expression. Familiarity with the text is no less essential in understanding the puppets' gestures, or what has occasioned the sudden sharpness of the samisen's tone. An acquaintance with past interpretations of the parts by the same or different artists also adds much to an appreciation of a new performance. Apart from such general considerations, the special characteristics of Bunraku require study too: the choice of head used for each character, the costuming, the patterns of gesture, the manner in which the Bunraku and Kabuki versions of the same play differ. A knowledge of the history of the art and techniques of Bunraku, though not indispensable to the enjoyment of a performance, also increases one's pleasure and understanding. It is hoped that the following chapters and the photographs will help to suggest the pleasures of Bunraku, though of course like all dramatic arts it can be fully appreciated only in the theatre.

II. THE HISTORY OF BUNRAKU

THE PUPPETS

Bunraku, the familiar name of the Japanese puppet theatre today, is a term dating back no further than the early nineteenth century. The art of puppetry, however, has been known in Japan for over a thousand years, though accounts in the old records are so cryptic that little can be said with confidence about its ancient history. Scholars have mulled over each word in the available evidence, and depending on their interpretations of the linguistic, folkloristic and literary materials, have reached quite different conclusions about the beginnings of puppetry in Japan. Some are convinced that the Japanese puppets were indigenous; others insist that they were introduced from abroad; and still others have attempted to find place for both native and foreign traditions.

The earliest Japanese name for "puppet" was *kugutsu*, a word found in an eighth-century gloss on a Chinese Buddhist text. This mysterious name has intrigued scholars for centuries; it has variously been traced to a Chinese word for puppet, pronounced approximately *kuai-luai-tzu* in the same period, or to *kuki* or *kukli*, gypsy words which some claim were probably the origin of both Chinese and Japanese terms. The Turkish *kukla*, and the late Greek *koukla* have also been cited as proof of the transmission of the art of puppetry from Asia Minor across the vast Central Asian regions to China, Korea, and eventually to Japan.

The possibility of foreign origins is intriguing, but the evidence is by no means conclusive. Japanese folklorists tend to reject such theories, pointing out that the sounds *kugu* or *kugutsu* are found in native shrine and deity names, a clue perhaps to some connection between the earliest puppets and religious worship at particular Shinto shrines. Puppets preserved today at shrines in scattered areas of Japan clearly suggest ancient traditions behind them. In the north, the worship of the god Oshira involves a medium who recites spells and stories accompanied by the two simple stick puppets she operates, one in each hand, raising, lowering, or confronting the puppets as she speaks. At two shrines in Kyushu, puppets, perhaps the oldest in Japan, perform dances and wrestling matches as part of the annual festival. These Shinto puppets are not representations of divinities (in the manner of Buddhist or Christian images) but, rather, wooden creatures temporarily "possessed" by the gods whose actions they recreate, much as the medium herself is believed to repeat, when "possessed," words uttered by the god himself. Puppet performances at a shrine are intended to depict deeds of the ancient past in order that men of later ages may know the glory of the divinity worshipped there. It is easy to imagine a purely indigenous art of puppetry developing from the sacred dolls used by mediums, but until the mystery of the name *kugutsu* is solved we cannot deny the possibility that puppet performances, introduced from abroad, were adopted in ancient times to Shinto worship.

What may have begun as fragmentary, incoherent utterances of a medium, accompanied by the rudimentary gestures of puppets, in time acquired a ritual and even dramatic form. Puppet plays (like sacred dances at Shinto shrines today) were probably offered to the gods by rich patrons in the hope of inducing them to grant additional prosperity. Because these performances were presented for the gods, human witnesses were unnecessary, but as the puppets came to attract spectators, an embryonic puppet theatre was created, and eventually, we may suppose, the pleasure of these spectators, as well as of the gods, was taken into consideration by the puppeteers. The simple movements of a stick puppet operated by a medium intoning ancient legends are, of course, a far cry from the sophisticated art of Bunraku, but even in its most primitive form we can detect one peculiar feature of the Japanese puppet theatre: the medium makes no attempt to conceal the fact that she is manipulating the puppets. Unlike puppet or marionette performances in other countries, then, the Japanese art normally did not require the illusion that the puppets were moving and speaking of their own accord.

The early history of Japanese puppetry might be interpreted entirely in terms of a spontaneous, native development, but probably continental influence was present even in the earliest stages. Certainly other entertainments, notably the comic *gigaku* and more stately *bugaku* dances, had been introduced to Japan from Korea and China by the seventh and eighth centuries. As in later times, one variety of theatrical performance could easily influence another: *gigaku* and *bugaku* masks and costumes may have contributed to the appearance of the primitive Japanese puppets. But this is no more than conjecture; it is more important to remember that dances ultimately originating in such distant regions as India and Central Asia were well known to the Japanese of the eighth century. It is likely too that along with these dances, humbler forms of entertainment, including puppetry, were introduced from abroad.

The oldest description of the Japanese puppeteers was written by the court scholar Ōe Masafusa (1041–1111). Though only 320 characters long, it has been scrutinized with desperate care by scholars of the Japanese theatre as the best source of information on the activities of these early puppeteers. It begins, "The puppeteers have no permanent place of residence nor fixed abodes, but live in tents. They move about freely, wherever there is water or grass; their customs much resemble those of the northern barbarians." Ōe's statement suggests that the puppeteers were not merely traveling entertainers but led a nomadic life, moving their beasts from place to place, depending on the supply of water and pasture. No other record indicates the existence of such nomads in Japan, and some scholars have therefore asserted that Ōe Masafusa merely used stock phraseology borrowed from Chinese accounts of foreign tribes to decorate his brief account of the puppeteers. Undoubtedly the choice of words was influenced by Chinese examples, but we cannot disregard Ōe's general implication that the puppeteers led lives so unlike those of the sedentary Japanese that they were taken for foreigners.

Ōe's account continues, "The men all use bows and horses, and make their living at hunting. Sometimes they fight with two swords or juggle balls; sometimes they make wooden puppets dance or peachwood puppets fight. These puppets faithfully depict the actions of living people. The puppeteers are almost as adept as the Chinese practitioners of magical transformations, and can change sand and stones into gold coins, or grass and wood into birds and beasts, cleverly deceiving the spectators' eyes." The main occupation of the puppeteers would seem thus to have been hunting, and their artistic talent only a secondary source of income, but this talent set them apart from other hunters and even other Japanese.

Ōe Masafusa turned his attention next to the womenfolk of the puppeteers. He tells us that they painted their faces, performed songs and dances, and enticed travelers to spend the night with them. The account concludes with the statement that the puppeteers, not being cultivators of the land, owed no allegiance to the local officials and showed no respect for the governors of the provinces where they lived. Immunity from taxation was the supreme joy of their lives; by way of thanks they worshipped their gods at night with much noisemaking.

Ōe Masafusa, in the interests of literary embellishment, may have exaggerated the rootlessness of the puppeteers. Documentary evidence indicates that as early as the twelfth century, puppeteers were in fact more or less permanently domiciled in different parts of the country, and owed some form of allegiance to the local rulers. It is nevertheless difficult to imagine that Ōe would have taken such pains to suggest that the puppeteers were aliens if, as some scholars claim, they were merely runaways from their normal ties to a particular domain. Their identity, like the origin of the word *kugutsu*, remains a mystery, but there is the strong inference that they migrated to Japan from the continent, bringing with them their art. Chinese records mention no such tribe of wandering puppeteers, but strikingly similar accounts are found in the Korean histories, which trace the *yangsuch'ŏk* as far back as the tenth century. Korean traditions, though no less vague than the Japanese, indicate that these entertainers, an outcaste group, were originally from Central Asia; the men, it would appear, on occasion operated puppets, and the women were witches and fortune-tellers. A Middle Korean word for puppet, *kuktu*, is tantalizingly close to *kugutsu*, but it has not yet been possible to prove the connection. The curiously gypsy-like attributes of both Japanese and Korean entertainers lend an intriguing note to the early history of puppetry in the Far East.

Accounts of performances by *kugutsu* say little about either their content or techniques. Clearly, however, the puppets were hand-operated, and not mechanical dolls of the kind so highly developed in China by the tenth century. The latter, described in Chinese records as early as the third century A.D., were originally introduced "from the West," and may indeed have been descended from the toys of ancient Egypt and Greece. Even if the Chinese first learned of such toys from the West, they quickly developed mechanical apparatuses far more sophisticated than those of their prototypes. An account from the early fourth century tells of a master doll-maker who fashioned a wooden room with a tiny housewife inside. When someone knocked on the door, the housewife would open it, come outside, bow, return to her room and shut the door. Another, even more complicated set of dolls was set in motion by four or five mice jumping on a kind of treadmill. The fondness of the Chinese court for these dolls led to increasingly realistic creations, including a doll which could pour wine with appropriate decorum at state banquets. It became a common cliché in describing these dolls to say that they were "exactly like human beings."

Evidence suggests that Chinese mechanical dolls were carried to Japan, perhaps as early as the tenth century, but the Japanese apparently lacked the technical skill either to create new devices or to repair old ones, and these expensive toys were presumably discarded once their mechanism failed. A description of a mechanical doll may be found in the *Konjaku Monogatari*, a late twelfth-century collection of stories. We are told how Prince Kaya in the ninth century, as part of a scheme to relieve a severe drought in Kyoto, built a mechanical doll over four feet high, which held buckets in both hands, and erected it in a field. When a bucket was filled with water, the doll would dash it over his face, so delighting spectators that they brought water from distant places in order to watch the doll perform. The fields were in no time amply watered and the drought relieved. The story, unfortunately for historians of Japanese puppetry, is of Chinese origin, and no other source indicates that the Japanese were capable of making such dolls before the fourteenth or fifteenth century.

The puppets used by the *kugutsu* were certainly more primitive than the Chinese mechanical dolls, but they were better suited to dramatic performances. No matter how complicated a series of movements a doll may perform, it cannot improvise beyond that series, and it is incapable of sustained actions. The *kugutsu* performances probably consisted originally of sword-play (as Ōe Masafusa mentioned) or wrestling (still performed today at the Kohyō Shrine in Kyushu), but eventually short dramas with more or less improvised dialogue spoken by the operators made up the *kugutsu* entertainments. An eleventh-century account describes a puppet play performed at a Shinto shrine during the course of which an aged man, after exchanging amorous words with his young wife, engages her in sexual intercourse. The spectators, men and women alike, were so amused that they "could not help cracking their jaws and splitting their sides with laughter." The salacious nature of this skit accords poorly with the holy precincts of a shrine but, as the account concludes, "Attending these performances brings two benefits: first, the spectator may worship the divine authority of the gods; second, he enjoys a pleasant relaxation."

Kugutsu performances undoubtedly were considered primarily as part of religious ceremonies held at a shrine; their amusement value was only incidental. Most puppet plays probably described in serious terms the history of a shrine or the miracles attributed to the deity worshiped there, perhaps in the manner of the Nō plays on similar subjects. Nothing suggests that, as in the later puppet theatre, plays were enacted to a text recited by a narrator. Puppets were preferred to actors as performers of the divine legends because they lacked the "smell" of human beings and could therefore impart mystery and authority to their gestures. The puppeteering techniques, as judged by later standards, must have been extremely crude, but probably characteristic human gestures were reproduced with sufficient fidelity to cause the spectators to say, in the traditional phrase, that the puppets seemed to be alive.

Despite the promise of a theatre worthy of the otherwise extremely literary and sophisticated world of eleventh-century Japan, the puppet entertainments offered by the *kugutsu*, far from developing with the years, suddenly cease to figure in the surviving documents. The name *kugutsu* occurs occasionally in legal records and elsewhere, but without any indication that persons known by that name were concerned with puppets. The *kugutsu* men, though generally domiciled on some manor, where they cultivated the land, were exempt from the usual taxes; they also sometimes engaged in hunting, as in the old days, or hired their services as laborers. The women were out-and-out prostitutes—the name *kugutsu* came to mean only "prostitute"—who worked in brothels situated along the principal thoroughfares. Some *kugutsu* with a lingering fondness for their art may have privately continued to operate puppets, or may have performed in regions not covered by existing records, but this remains conjectural.

A revival of puppetry occurred in the fourteenth century, apparently as a result of the importation of string-operated marionettes from China. A poem by the Buddhist monk Ryōsai (died 1365) is entitled "Puppets" (*Kairai*):

> They turn like toys in automatic movements,
> But their actions, filled with marvelous life, do not cease.
> A single string brings us a bodhisattva's face;
> An inch of thread tugs away a yaksha's head.

Mention of toys in the first line indicates that mechanical dolls, at least of a crude sort, existed in Japan at the time. The marionettes moved like these dolls, but unlike toys, their performance did not stop when the mechanism ran down. Mention of a single string operating a marionette dressed as a bodhisattva is probably not to be taken literally; at least three or four strings attached to the head, arms, and torso would be required to achieve any artistic effect. "An inch of thread" suggests that only a short distance separated the marionette's head from the platform above which the operator manipulated the strings. These meager clues have been interpreted as meaning that the marionettes were no more than a foot tall and that they moved on a stage about three feet wide and a foot and a half high. Probably only one or two marionettes appeared on the stage at a time, and the plays, like similar ones in China, dealt with Buddhist descriptions of heaven and hell.

Marionettes never attracted the Japanese as much as stick puppets. Although they enjoyed periods of popularity in the following centuries and survive today in a few rural temples as regional entertainments, they failed to achieve any great artistic development. The introduction of marionettes from China, however, apparently led to a reawakening of interest in the native forms of puppetry, which may have survived (as almost every form of Japanese theatrical entertainment known to us by name has survived to the present day) in remote areas, practiced by amateurs rather than by professional *kugutsu*.

In the fifteenth century, especially, the importation of Chinese mechanical dolls (as part of the Shogun Yoshimitsu's mania for things Chinese) stirred Japanese craftsmen into imitations and refinements. Some devices were operated by strings, others by using water power, and they became increasingly complex. By 1579, to cite one example, a mechanical toy was invented which set in motion 2000 soldiers in a battle for control of a castle six feet square. The manufacturer and operation of such mechanical toys came to be considered the speciality of the outcaste (*eta*) class, which otherwise figures most importantly in the history of the Japanese theatre. In 1461, we are told, the Shogun Yoshimasa visited an outcaste village to the west of Kyoto especially to see some mechanical dolls perform. The use of such dolls on festival floats began about this time and continues to this day.

In the middle of sixteenth century, with the arrival of Christian missionaries from Europe, new varieties of mechanical toys were introduced. A letter from a Portuguese missionary in the province of Bungo, written in 1562 to his superior in the Society of Jesus at home, describes a performance at Easter: "We showed them such scenes from the Bible as the children of Israel leaving Egypt. We constructed a Red Sea and made it open to permit the passage of the Israelites, and close when Pharaoh crossed with his troops. We also showed the prophet Jonah emerging from the whale's belly and other scenes."

Neither the Chinese nor the European mechanical dolls had any major influence on the subsequent development of the puppet theatre in Japan, but in one respect at least these toys may have been important: the use of strings inside the puppet to manipulate its eyes, mouth, and fingers (as opposed to external strings used with marionettes) may have been suggested by the strings which set in motion the mechanical dolls. A poem by the celebrated monk Ikkyū (1398-1481) gives a philosophical interpretation of the puppets:

> The puller of strings is himself the chief actor,
> As earth and water unite at the will of fire and air.
> When the play on the stage has ended,
> The setting suddenly is empty again.

The poem apparently means that a puppet, though it seems to move independently, is but the external manifestation of the operator's will, just as the visible phenomena of the world obey the invisible influences of fire and air. When the play has ended, and the guiding spirit no longer exerts its will, the stage—and the world—suddenly reverts to emptiness. In another poem on the puppets, Ikkyū relates that they perform so successfully as nobles or commoners that the spectator forgets they are merely wooden figures, and wonders if they are not actually human.

Ikkyū's poems are obscurely worded, and we cannot be sure that the strings he mentions operated puppets from inside, rather than marionettes from above, but the term he employs for stage suggests a puppet theatre. His mention of nobles and commoners is also too vague for us to guess the plots or even the general nature of the plays, but we know from other sources that by the middle of the fifteenth century puppets were used to perform Nō dramas and Kyōgen farces. It is hard to imagine the effect of the stately, symbolic Nō dramas when performed by crude little puppets, but the Nō and Kyōgen plays constituted the only available repertory, and the puppeteers accordingly continued to perform them for centuries. In 1614, for example, a program combining one play written especially for the puppets and several Nō plays was presented at the palace. In the middle of the seventeenth century, programs of Nō plays alternating with puppet plays were offered, but the audiences so much preferred the latter that before long the Nō plays were relegated to the intermissions. The development of an adequate repertory of puppet plays was, however, a slow process, and for many years the works performed either belonged to another theatre or were merely crude exhibitions of the puppeteers' skill.

Developments immediately before the emergence in the late sixteenth century of a puppet theatre worthy of the name are closely connected with the activities of the *ebisu-kaki*. These operators apparently originally served as menials at the Ebisu Shrine at Nishinomiya but learned the art of puppetry from outcastes in order to present legends concerning the god Ebisu. In 1555, as contemporary accounts relate, four *ebisu-kaki* staged a performance of Nō, attracting such attention that from this time on puppet performers, despite their base origins, were frequently invited to the palace. When peace was restored in 1600 after centuries of warfare, the services of *ebisu-kaki* were widely in demand at shrines and temples throughout the country. Eventually they broke their connections with the Ebisu Shrine in Nishinomiya, and were absorbed into the newly created puppet theatre, but the word *ebisu* continued to possess the meaning of "puppet," as we know from the *ebisu-mai* (or "*ebisu* dances"), the miniature puppet shows of the late seventeenth century. Pictures of the *ebisu-mai* show the operators with a box which served as a stage slung from their necks. One woodcut shows two operators, each carrying a box fashioned like a tiny Nō stage complete with a roof, who stand side by side, about a foot apart. The stages, about sixteen inches square, have no floor; instead, the puppets are held up at stage level from beneath by the operators, their hands concealed by the base of the stage. The effect of a single play performed on two separated stages is hard to imagine, but perhaps only Nō dances were attempted. Later examples of *ebisu-mai* stages were less elaborate, but strings were employed to advantage in manipulating the arms and legs of the puppets, by this time about eight inches high.

One further variety of late sixteenth-century puppet entertainment was the *hotoke-mawashi* or "Buddha turning," which (judging from illustrations) resembled the *ebisu-kaki*, but used hand-puppets a foot and a half tall. Unlike the *ebisu-kaki*, however, *hotoke-mawashi* was associated primarily with Buddhist temples instead of Shinto shrines, and it is supposed that the operators acted out Buddhist texts and sermons. The nearest surviving examples of such puppets are those manipulated by mediums of the Oshira cult (described above) in reciting the legend of the gallant horse Kurige and his love, the Princess Tamayo, who eventually became the gods of silkworm cultivation. The Oshira puppets, first mentioned in 1598, are moved in a stiff, ritualistic manner well suited to the monotonous recitation. Their actions possess only slight representational or dramatic interest, for the performance is considered a sacred rite, not a play designed to please an audience. This may also have been the purpose of the early *hotoke-mawashi*, but gradually the sermons developed into plays. If, like the Oshira puppets, the *hotoke-mawashi* plays combined puppets with a narrated text, they represented an important development in the direction of the future art of Bunraku. The puppet theatre was subsequently to present not plays in a Western sense (with texts divided into parts assigned to the different characters), but narratives which included in addition to the dialogue many descriptive passages assigned to no character, but recited by a chanter-commentator. In the earlier theatre the operator may have supplied dialogue for his puppet, as in some regional theatres today, but with the adoption of narrated texts all parts came to be taken by a chanter who modulated his voice suitably in assuming different roles or in describing a scene. The union between Buddhism and the puppets effected by the *hotoke-mawashi* is important otherwise because it prefigures the *sekkyō-bushi*, a kind of morality play acted by puppets which became popular in the seventeenth century. The religious and ritual significance of the early puppet theatre, whether Shintoist or Buddhist in coloring, remained of dominant importance until late in its development.

THE TALE IN TWELVE EPISODES OF JŌRURI

Puppet shows, as we have seen, had a history of perhaps eight hundred years behind them by the times of these events in the sixteenth century, but only with the creation of texts written especially for the puppets (and not merely adopted for puppet performance from some other medium) is it possible to speak of a puppet theatre, in the sense of the modern Bunraku. The puppets, of course, gave Bunraku its most distinctive feature, but the texts were to develop this theatre into a truly artistic medium, and to distinguish Bunraku from puppet and marionette entertainments elsewhere in the world. Even today, at the beginning of a Bunraku performance, the chanters lift the text to their foreheads to indicate respect; it would be unthinkable that, like actors, they would feel at liberty to add or delete phrases to suit their own tastes. Of the three elements in Bunraku —text, puppets, and musical accompaniment—the text is clearly the most important, and Bunraku thus fundamentally differs from Kabuki, where, even when a Bunraku text is performed, the actor is the center of interest and the text hardly more than a vehicle. As the person closest to the text, the chanter *(tayū)* ranks above the samisen players and puppet operators, and though there have been musicians and operators whose exceptional talents have dominated a company, the chanter, the servant of the text, more frequently gives the performance his personal cachet.

Bunraku, though a form of puppet show, and in this sense comparable to similar entertainments in other countries, whether the marionettes of Europe or the shadow plays of China and Java, is basically a narrative art. The chanter declaims the story, altering his voice in the dialogue to suggest the tones of a warrior, a woman, or a child, and at times, in poetical passages, rising from speech to song. But he is neither an actor nor a singer, but a storyteller. Ideally perhaps, he should not be visible at all, but Japanese audiences prefer to see the narrator, though his presence destroys the illusion that the puppets, for all the movements of their mouths, are speaking for themselves. The celebrated chanters have enjoyed great popularity; audiences delight in the extraordinary range of expression which crosses their faces, and in the tears which fall from their eyes in tragic scenes. Indeed, in some parts of Japan performances are preferred of the chanters alone without the puppets, as if the latter were an unnecessary or even undesirable addition to a master chanter's rendering of the text. The Bunraku plays, it need hardly be said, are written specifically for a narrator rather than for actors, as one can tell immediately from the almost invariable addition of such concluding phrases as "thus he spoke" or "he said with a smile." These comments are natural in a narrative, but would be unnecessary in a theatre of actors. Bunraku, then, is a form of storytelling, recited to a musical accompaniment, and embodied by puppets on a stage.

The history of Bunraku may be traced back in different directions, depending on the focus of one's interests. Up to this point I have considered it mainly as a form of puppet theatre, and have therefore discussed early puppeteers rather than the chanters or samisen players. But if we turn our attention to the antecedents for the texts, a different series of events must be reported, and the same is true of the samisen. The confluence of three different performing traditions in the middle of the sixteenth century created the art of Bunraku.

Bunraku, as has been mentioned, is a modern term. The older designation for the art was *jōruri*, the name of the heroine of a fifteenth-century romance usually called "The Tale in Twelve Episodes of Jōruri" *(Jōruri-Jūnidan Sōshi)*. Although rewritten more artistically in later times, the text was essentially a narrative meant to be recited by professional storytellers. Like "The Tale of the Heike" *(Heike Monogatari)*, its thirteenth-century predecessor, "The Tale in Twelve Episodes" was altered and expanded by successive storytellers, who recited the text to the accompaniment of the musical instrument (rather resembling the mandolin) called the *biwa*. At a time when other entertainments were scarce, villagers delighted in hearing even for the hundredth time the storyteller's narration of the great deeds which occurred during the warfare between the Taira and the Minamoto, especially the more pathetic and lyrical episodes. The *biwa*, a melodious instrument, provided a kind of musical comment on the narrated passages (rather like the harpsichord during the recitatives of a Mozart opera), and was not an accompaniment to the narrator's voice in the manner of the samisen of later years. The narrator's delivery was rhythmical, and sometimes rose to musical expression; in order to emphasize the rhythm, he beat time with a fan. We may suppose that each storyteller had favorite sections of this long work which displayed his particular talents to best advantage. He might eventually augment such episodes from "The Tale of the Heike" with additional material from other traditional sources or of his own invention. His audiences, like those in India today for recitations of the Sanskrit epics, enjoyed the poetic language even though it is difficult at times to understand, and apparently never tired of hearing about its heroes. By the middle of the fifteenth century, however, recitations of the original "Tale of the Heike" waned in popularity, and other stories about the same heroes, particularly the gallant Yoshitsune, became the staples of the storytellers' repertory. "The Tale in Twelve Episodes" belongs to this category.

The story is a jumble of fantastic and believable events, which neither in style nor in incidents remotely approaches the grandeur of "The Tale of the Heike." Listeners, however, undoubtedly welcomed the romantic treatment of the hero. Yoshitsune, accompanied by a retainer, leaves the capital for the Eastern Provinces. While journeying through the province of Mikawa he catches a glimpse of a peerlessly beautiful lady and falls in love at first sight. Later, when this lady is making music with her companions, Yoshitsune, outside her gate, joins in with his flute, playing so beautifully that Jōruri invites him into the house. Yoshitsune goes that night to Jōruri's room, and after much persuasion induces her to yield her favors. As they are sorrowfully parting the next morning, Jōruri's mother surprises them together, and the disconcerted Yoshitsune flees. When he reaches the strand of Fukiage he is stricken with a mysterious, wasting sickness, and seems at the point of death when Shō-Hachiman, the protective deity of his family, appears in the guise of an old priest and offers to bring help from the capital. Yoshitsune requests that Jōruri be summoned instead, and the god, complying with his wish, appears the next instant before Jōruri's maid and informs her of Yoshitsune's illness. Jōruri and the maid rush to Fukiage, and after much difficulty they find the cottage where Yoshitsune lies dying. At first it seems they have arrived too late, but after Jōruri has purified herself in the sea and prayed to all the gods and Buddhas of Japan for Yoshitsune's recovery, tears falling from her eyes into his mouth revive the dying man. At this point sixteen mountain priests mysteriously appear, and by dint of their prayers and spells Yoshitsune recovers. Once restored to health he must leave again on the journey, in order that he may fulfill his destiny of one day destroying the Heike. The lovers part in grief, with vows of meeting again.

Though "The Tale in Twelve Episodes" includes such charming scenes as the description of Yoshitsune falling in love at first sight with Jōruri, it is puzzling why this particular, essentially inartistic story should have continued to please successive audiences for almost a century or why, for that matter, a work with so few dramatic incidents should have furnished the puppet theatre with its first text. We must not forget, however, the extraordinary popularity of the legends about Yoshitsune, the closest Japanese approximation to an epic hero. Even the Catholic missionaries at the end of the sixteenth century chose "The Tale of the Heike" as the most suitable text for teaching Japanese to beginners and prepared an edition in roman letters. Sections from "The Tale of the Heike" had been employed almost unaltered in the Nō theatre, where the prevailingly gloomy tone, stressing the tragic brevity and uncertainty of life, was entirely appropriate and could be appreciated by the aristocratic audience. The puppet theatre, however, aimed at plebeian spectators, and therefore naturally preferred the more romantic Yoshitsune of "The Tale in Twelve Episodes." Successive texts of the Jōruri story show moreover a tendency to emphasize episodes especially suited to performance, and to omit less dramatic parts. As early as 1531, as we know from the diary kept by the poet Sōchō, blind storytellers were "singing" the story of Jōruri, and by the end of the sixteenth century the name Jōruri had come to designate not merely the character in the romance, but a particular variety of entertainment provided by the storytellers. By the latter part of the sixteenth century, *jōruri* recitations had attained extraordinary popularity in Kyoto; a list of popular entertainments offered in 1592 is headed by *jōruri*.

THE FUSION OF THE THREE ELEMENTS OF BUNRAKU

There are many legends but little documentary evidence concerning the manner in which puppets and the samisen were joined to the narration of the *jōruri*. Our earliest records go back to about 1600, when, as part of a special entertainment offered in Kyoto, *ebisu-kaki* puppeteers were invited to perform in conjunction with *jōruri* recitations. The combination proved such a success that similar programs were later arranged. An entry in a nobleman's diary for 1614 tells us: "Rain. Went to the palace. After dinner they performed a play called "The Chest-Splitting of Amida" (*Amida no Munewari*). Players of the *ebisu-kaki* variety attended, and put on a performance after first setting up a curtain in the palace garden. It was most extraordinary. They also performed *Kamo, Daibutsu Kuyō, Takasago*, and other Nō plays." The performance was staged by command of the Retired Emperor Goyōzei, whose interest in the art was so great that some sources credit him with having first suggested that puppets be employed to perform the story of Jōruri. His son, the Emperor Gomizunō, is believed to have begun the practice of bestowing honorary court ranks on the outstanding performers. Such evidence of imperial interest in the fledgling puppet theatre is tantalizingly incomplete, but it is clear at least from the nobleman's diary that by 1614 not only were puppets commonly joined to the narration, but new works had been composed to take the place of the overly familiar story of Princess Jōruri.

The samisen was apparently introduced to Japan from the Ryukyu Islands before 1570. An account for 1575 relates how natives of the Ryukyus appeared before the daimyo of Satsuma, and sang to the accompaniment of a *"jabisen."* The name was written with characters which mean "snakeskin strings," though snakeskin was in fact used not for the strings but for covering the body of the instrument. A similar three-stringed instrument is still played in South China, undoubtedly the source of the Ryukyu *jabisen*. The name was quickly modified in Japan to shamisen or samisen, and came to be written usually with characters meaning "three-flavor strings." Before long the snakeskin covering gave way to catskin, both because snakeskins of the appropriate size were rare in Japan, and because the Japanese played the samisen so vigorously, in the traditions of the *biwa*, that the plectrum was likely to damage snakeskin. Catskin was not only more durable but produced a clearer, harder tone which made it an ideal instrument for accompanying the recitations.

At first the Japanese, ever eager for curiosities from abroad, prized the samisen mainly as a novelty, and it was played by female entertainers especially. Its popularity is attested by mentions in lists of entertainments from the late sixteenth century, but nothing suggests the samisen had already been combined with the *jōruri* recitations which figured in the same programs. Probably "modern" *biwa* accompanists experimented for a time with the samisen, as in the late nineteenth century violins were tried out as background music for Kabuki plays, without any decision being made for or against adopting the new instrument. Later, as the expressive capacities of the samisen were improved, accompanists found that its sharp, almost percussive notes were ideally suited to guiding the narrator in his delivery and the operators in maneuvering the puppets. The difference in effect between the *biwa* and the samisen when used as an accompaniment is comparable to the difference between accompanying a singer with a violin or a piano.

Once the three elements of Bunraku had at last been joined, the combination began to seem inevitable. A performance then as now was guided first of all by the text, which chanters, samisen players and puppeteers studied alike in the hopes of bringing out its full meaning in their various domains. The mutual dependence of the three elements is so great that we can hardly imagine Bunraku in any other terms, but our knowledge of the puppet theatre in the early seventeenth century, imperfect as it is, suggests that what now seems so inevitable probably was largely accidental in the first instance, and only with time and the gradual perfection of each of the three branches of the art did the ideal interdependence, so often mentioned by admirers of Bunraku, acquire its present meaning.

Paintings from the early seventeenth century give us valuable indications about the nature of the performances. A screen painted about 1622 shows two tiny puppet theatres in operation. The theatres themselves seem hardly able to hold twenty-five people each—men and women, clearly of the plebeian class, who watch with gaping mouths a stage at one side of the rectangular enclosure. The puppets are held up over a cloth-covered partition by the operators, who are invisible below. The puppets are small, apparently only about a foot tall, and have no arms, though in some cases the kimono sleeves are held at angles to suggest arms (as in modern Bunraku the feet for female puppets are delineated by the hems of her kimono). One of the two puppet theatres depicted on the screen belongs to the normal *jōruri* tradition. Neither chanter nor musical accompanist is visible, in keeping with practice at the time. The other theatre probably is performing *sekkyō-bushi*, a didactic, Buddhist-inspired puppet play which originated almost contemporaneously with *jōruri* in the early seventeenth century, and for a century was its rival in popular favor. Two men seated to the left of the stage in the *sekkyō-bushi* theatre, though partly concealed by a wall, seem to be the chanter and his accompanist, an indication that their appearance before the audience antedated this practice in *jōruri*. But, of course, a screen painting is not necessarily to be trusted as an accurate representation of theatres at the time.

Our earliest extended description of a *jōruri* performance comes from the pen of Hayashi Razan (1573–1657), a Confucian philosopher who attended a performance in 1648. He described a variety of wooden puppets—men, women, monks, laity, immortals, soldiers, and so on—which danced, propelled boats, skirmished in battle (with heads flying), and executed various prodigies of transformation. He praised the chief operator, Koheita, then considered to be the most accomplished puppeteer in Edo, and concluded his description in the time-honored manner by declaring that the puppets seemed to be alive. We may doubt that the crude puppets which Koheita held up over his head and manipulated in the movements of dancing or fighting could really have induced anyone to believe they were alive, but compared to earlier, even cruder performances, Koheita's probably seemed remarkably vivid.

It appears likely that when puppets first accompanied the narration of the story of Jōruri their motions were intended not to embody the meaning of the texts (as in later times) but rather to create pleasing visual effects complementary to the narration. Thus, a passage in "The Tale in Twelve Episodes" utterly devoid of action might, particularly if the language lent itself to lyrical declamation, provide a suitable background for a dance, much as the recitations of the Nō chorus often provide the setting for a dance whose movements may be virtually unrelated to the circumstances described in the texts. Early *jōruri* performances were certainly heavily dependent on examples from the Nō, if only because the puppeteers customarily also performed Nō plays, as has been mentioned. The development of *jōruri* as a theatre whose texts were directly and even literally reflected in the actions of the stage was to mark a notable shift of direction in Japanese dramatic techniques. Perhaps Hayashi Razan, remembering the stylized, remote movements of the Nō plays, was more struck by the realism of the puppet theatre than a modern audience would be.

The art of *jōruri* showed a steady development during the course of the seventeenth century, mainly in the use of increasingly artistic texts and a correspondingly artistic manner of delivery by the chanters. Most of the early *jōruri* plays depended heavily on supernatural and miraculous elements, as we might have expected in works derived largely from Buddhist and Shinto sources. ("The Tale in Twelve Episodes," though the earliest *jōruri*, included comparatively few supernatural elements because of its secular origins.) The activities of ghosts, dragons, and foxes, so much admired by Razan, illustrate one advantage the puppets held over actors, whose physical limitations made convincing miracles difficult to achieve onstage. The puppeteers naturally exploited this advantage, either by using mechanical dolls *(karakuri)*, some of which could be operated by remote control with the use of long strings, or else by allowing their puppets a freedom from gravity and the other earthly controls that prevent actors from achieving feats of superhuman quality. The poorly educated audiences had an enormous appetite for such stunts, and even a master dramatist like Chikamatsu, who had no need to rely on tricks in his plays, was obliged at times to yield to this craving for the miraculous.

The names of the major chanters of the seventeenth century are important because each man contributed a distinctive style of narration, usually known by his name. The chanters were responsible for reducing the original twelve episodes of the *jōruri* story to the six acts of the early *jōruri* play, and for later further reducing this number to five, probably influenced by the number of Nō plays presented in a single program. An equation was made between the five acts of the *jōruri* and the five Nō plays of a program, and the same progression of tempo was demanded, going from the expository solemnity (*jo*) of the first two plays (or acts of *jōruri*) to the intenser, more broken emotions (*ha*) of the next two plays, and finally to a climax in the furious tempo (*kyū*) of the concluding work. Expressed in terms of plot, the first act was usually devoted to a description of the villainy which gives rise to the play. The second act shows virtue beginning to assert itself even amidst the triumph of evil. In the third act, the advantage shifts to the side of virtue, thanks to some deed of self-sacrifice. The fourth act depicts the struggle between virtue and vice, culminating in the triumph of virtue, and in the fifth act, usually the shortest, the annihilation of the original villainy is celebrated. Undoubtedly the *jōruri* equivalent of the programs of five Nō plays represents a debasement or at least a popularization of the lofty aesthetic ideals of Nō, but the presence, even in this form, of influence from the aristocratic Nō drama not only fostered the development of *jōruri* considerably as a literary art, but caused the texts to be embellished with quotations from both the Nō and the poetry of an even more distant past. It served also to distinguish the puppet theatre from Kabuki, an art which sprang into being at almost exactly the same time as *jōruri*, and remained its close rival for two hundred years. Bunraku, despite its humble origins and its continued dependence on a virtually illiterate public in the countryside as well as the cities, acquired, by borrowing from Nō, a literary importance which Kabuki, always more dependent on the skill and personality of the great actors than on the text, would never possess.

Bunraku, like Kabuki, had its inception in Kyoto, but developed during the early seventeenth century most conspicuously in Edo. The people of this new city, populated largely by samurai and other persons unfamiliar with the traditional Kyoto culture, welcomed the vigorous rhythms of the new *jōruri* works, particularly those dealing with the adventures of the incomparable martial hero Kimpira. The chanter of these plays, Satsuma Jōun (1595–1672), whose renditions of the Kimpira stories enjoyed immense popularity in Edo, is reported to have beat time with an iron bar, the better to maintain the fierce atmosphere of the plots. Satsuma Jōun is otherwise credited with having been the first to reduce the twelve episodes of the original Jōruri story to six acts of *jōruri*. The popularity of the Kimpira plays spread to other parts of the country, even to Kyoto, where the gloomily moral *sekkyō-bushi* was firmly entrenched. Bunraku might, however, have remained predominantly an Edo theatrical art had it not been for the disastrous Great Fire of Edo of 1657, which killed more than 100,000 people and destroyed most of the city. As a result of the fire, the leading chanters, despairing of making a living in the ruined city, moved to the Osaka and Kyoto area; from this time onwards Bunraku ceased to be of great importance to Edo, where Kabuki instead was to reign supreme.

Ever since the late seventeenth century Bunraku has been associated especially with the city of Osaka. Scholars have often asserted that this fact reflects the commercial temper of Osaka, as opposed to the bravado of Edo or the refinement of Kyoto, but they fail to indicate what precisely in puppet performances would appeal especially to merchants. It is probably safer to explain the persistent popularity of Bunraku in Osaka, even when it had lost ground elsewhere, as a historical accident—a fortunate one, for any art firmly entrenched in the commercial metropolis of Japan enjoyed financial security. Under the patronage of the Osaka audiences, Bunraku developed rapidly in the mid-seventeenth century.

THE GOLDEN AGE OF BUNRAKU

The celebrated chanter Takemoto Gidayū (1651–1714) established the Takemoto Theatre in 1684 on the Dōtombori, a street of theatres, restaurants, and other places of entertainment in Osaka. The first work that he presented was the historical play "The Soga Heir" (*Yotsugi Soga*) by Chikamatsu Monzaemon (1653–1725), the greatest of the *jōruri* playwrights. The auspicious combination of two geniuses was to impart true drama to what had frequently been moralistic or else coarse forms of entertainment. The production of "Kagekiyo Victorious" (*Shusse Kagekiyo*), a *jōruri* by Chikamatsu in 1686, is considered to mark the beginning of the "new" *jōruri*; from this triumph the two men went on to effect startling improvements in the medium. Their key success was probably "The Love Suicides at Sonezaki" (*Sonezaki Shinjū*) in 1703. Its importance may be measured in financial terms, for it assured the fortunes of the Takemoto Theatre after some shaky years of poor attendance. It also determined Chikamatsu, who had been dividing his energies between Bunraku and Kabuki, to devote himself exclusively to the writing of *jōruri* texts for Gidayū. This decision was followed by his removal from Kyoto, still an important Kabuki center, to Osaka. Most importantly, the success of "The Love Suicides at Sonezaki," which describes in realistic fashion a young merchant of soy sauce who commits suicide with the prostitute he loves, led to the series of tragedies on which Chikamatsu's reputation as a dramatist is largely based. These plays, inspired by actual happenings known to the audience, differed enormously from the traditional *jōruri*, which delighted in describing the fantastic deeds of the ancient heroes. Instead of attempting to intrigue the spectators with the grotesque posturings of superhuman heroes or the miraculous interventions of the gods and Buddha, Chikamatsu sought in his domestic plays to depict on the stage (in fictionalized form, of course) the tragedies which occur in ordinary daily life, giving them stature by means of the beauty of his language and the stylization possible in a theatre of puppets. The earlier *jōruri* plays had exploited the capability of the puppets to represent feats beyond human powers, but in these intensely human works the function of the puppets is instead to lend artistic distinction to what otherwise might seem merely painful or even sordid occurrences.

Nevertheless, a constant progression in the direction of realism may be traced through the history of *jōruri*. Not only did the texts, particularly Chikamatsu's domestic plays, depict the lives of actual people more faithfully than earlier works, but the puppets and the techniques employed in manipulating them were constantly being improved with the aim of achieving greater resemblance to human behavior. The puppets in the older *jōruri* plays, like those found in certain regions of Japan today, had neither arms nor legs, but the operator might, for example, brandish a sword or fan by concealing his own right hand in the sleeve of the puppet's kimono (as in the screen painting of 1622). The puppets were not provided with functional arms until the 1690's, when a citizen of Osaka, declaring that the existing puppets were no better than childish toys—they consisted merely of heads stuck on frames draped with kimonos—contrived to add movable arms to the puppets. By 1727, the same year that it became possible to open or shut the eyes and mouths of the puppets, the puppets' fingers could be manipulated, and in 1733 the fingers were further improved to permit the first joints to move independently. These improvements in the puppets owed much to the rivalry persisting between the Takemoto Theatre (Gidayū's) and the Toyotake Theatre; each tried to attract customers by displaying some novelty the other as yet did not possess. The series of developments also represented a response to public demand for more convincing puppets.

We must not, however, ignore the balancing emphasis on non-realism. During the first performance of "The Love Suicides at Sonezaki," the scene of the lovers' journey to their suicide was performed with a translucent curtain instead of the usual wooden partition concealing the area underneath the stage; this permitted the audience to watch the operators manipulating the puppets. Two years later, in 1705, the performance of another play by Chikamatsu, "The Mirror of

Craftsmen of the Emperor Yōmei," marked the beginning of the tradition that Bunraku operators be fully visible. On this occasion too the chanters (who had hitherto remained concealed in the wings) appeared before the audience on a platform at the side of the stage. The personal popularity of the operator Tatsumatsu Hachirobei is sometimes cited to explain this change, which was presumably compounded by the jealousy of the chanters. Certainly Tatsumatsu's popularity was a contributing factor but, as I have mentioned, each step in the direction of realism tended to be accompanied by a step in the direction of non-realism; whether or not the audiences or performers were aware of this general truth, they may have sensed that an excessive emphasis on realism would force the theatre out of the slender margin between the real and unreal. In the earlier *jōruri* there had been no question of the theatrical, unreal natures of the performances, and it was appropriate therefore that the sources of the movements and voices of the puppet—the chanters and operators—remained concealed, lest all dramatic illusion be destroyed. But with the introduction of plays in which quite ordinary people spoke the familiar language of the gay quarters, the audiences welcomed the visible presence of operators and chanters, the better to distinguish between real life and the theatre. The adoption in 1734 of puppets operated by three men enabled Bunraku to attain subtleties of performance unrivaled by any similar company in the world, but it involved the conspicuous presence of three men around each puppet, a challenge to dramatic illusion too great perhaps for non-Japanese audiences to accept. A multifold combination of opposites characterizes Bunraku and accounts for much of its greatness.

The success of "The Love Suicides at Sonezaki" and other domestic tragedies did not cause Chikamatsu to abandon the composition of historical plays filled with displays of heroics. The domestic plays, being too short to constitute a full day at the theatre, could be performed only as a part of a program, usually at the end of a long historical play. "The Love Suicides at Sonezaki," his first domestic tragedy, was not divided into acts, but Chikamatsu's later works in this form were usually in three acts, each divided into scenes. The high point of the plays was the *michiyuki* or "journey," in which the lovers travel together, often to the place where they will commit a double suicide. The lyrical beauty of these episodes, contrasting with the realism of the previous scenes, supplied a welcome diversion, and the magnificent poetry lavished by Chikamatsu in his descriptions imparted to the characters the stature necessary for them to command not only our pity but our admiration. Chikamatsu eventually came also to incorporate in his historical plays some scenes marked by the down-to-earth realism of the domestic tragedies. Most works of the heyday of *jōruri*, the mid-eighteenth century, belonged to a mixed genre which combined the excitement and extravagance of the historical plays with the pathos and humanity of the domestic tragedies. The couplings were not always smooth or entirely convincing, but they met the public demand for both realism and non-realism in the same work.

Chikamatsu's high reputation as a dramatist has saddled him with the unfortunate sobriquet "the Shakespeare of Japan." His plays, however, are seldom performed today by the Bunraku artists in their original form, a reflection in part of public preference for the kind of exaggerated expression more characteristic of later plays than those by Chikamatsu; by the standards of Chikamatsu's successors, his plays seem insufficiently engrossing or even pallid because of the scarcity of scenes featured by acts of self-immolation or by a retainer's sacrifice of his child to substitute for his master's. Sometimes these "deficiencies" in Chikamatsu's works have been remedied by extensive revision at the hands of later men, who have not hesitated to add melodramatic passages or surprise situations in an attempt to make Chikamatsu's works fit more smoothly into the pattern of later *jōruri*. The purist cannot but deplore such intrusions, which usually lower the dignity of a masterpiece, but in order to satisfy the public it was necessary for the Bunraku troupe to provide the puppets with more opportunity for display than Chikamatsu, in his concern for literary excellence, saw fit to supply.

A second difficulty in presenting Chikamatsu's text as originally composed is that he wrote for the kind of puppets used by Tatsumatsu Hachirobei—small, easily maneuvered creatures which were held up over the stage by the puppeteer working below. When the three-man puppet came into general use it was discovered that Chikamatsu's dialogue did not provide the slower, more cumbersome new puppets sufficient time to move through their parts. The lines had to be cut substantially if the plays were to be performed at all; but even this expedient was unsatisfactory, for the cut versions, unlike subsequent texts composed especially for the three-man puppets, offered no occasion for displaying the special realistic effects of which the new puppets were capable and which the public demanded.

A final difficulty arose from the tendency of the varieties of heads used in the puppet theatre to become increasingly rigid. The heads were divided not only into male and female, old and young, but also into good and evil. This meant inevitably that the nature of a character became apparent merely from his head as soon as he stepped on the stage—whether a good old man or a wicked middle-aged woman, and so on. There was little room for the individuality which Chikamatsu tried at times to impart to his portrayals. Surprising twists in the plot were not only possible but normal, as when Matsuōmaru in "The Village School" is revealed as having actually been loyal to his old master despite all appearances, or when we discover that Kumagai in "Kumagai's Camp" has killed his son to save his presumed enemy; but it was not possible to keep a character from being wholly good or wholly evil, or even to cause us to withhold judgment on his nature, as Chikamatsu sometimes attempted. In the revised versions of his texts the ambiguous characters become from the outset unmistakably good or evil.

The puppet theatre in the period from the death of Chikamatsu in 1725 to the 1780's enjoyed its greatest popularity, easily surpassing that of Kabuki, probably the only instance in theatrical history where puppets have been preferred to actors for such a long period. The supremacy of Bunraku was undisputed in Osaka, and in Edo, where Kabuki remained more popular, the actors felt obliged to borrow jōruri texts and even details of performance from the puppets. The later texts failed to equal Chikamatsu's in beauty of language or skill of construction (some of the most famous works, such as *Sugawara Denju Tenarai Kagami*, consist of a sprawling series of almost unrelated, though individually effective, scenes), but they showed an unparalleled mastery of the art of the puppet theatre. Just as a Kabuki play stands or falls in terms of the opportunities it affords the actors for displays of histrionics—moments when the actors can "really act"—so the jōruri came to depend on familiar but invariably effective display scenes for the puppets. In neither the Kabuki nor the later jōruri was literary excellence a principal objective, and although the language is often effective and even poetic, the plays usually lack the artistic finish which might enable them to survive as literature; these texts, in this respect, are more like opera libretti than like independent dramas. Most famous eighteenth-century works were written by three or more collaborators, each contributing an act or two in his special vein of excellence; sometimes, it would appear, little attempt was made by the different authors to reconcile the plots of their respective sections of the play. But although the literary value of these plays may be questionable, the authors knew exactly how to please the public, and their works have remained to this day the staples of the repertory.

A few of the post-Chikamatsu plays deserve to be treated as masterpieces, especially the celebrated *Chūshingura* (1748) by Takeda Izumo, Miyoshi Shōraku, and Namiki Sōsuke. This recounting of the vengeance executed by the forty-seven loyal retainers of the Lord of Akō, a fictionalized version of events which took place in Edo some forty-five years before, proved the most successful work ever written for puppets, and is still staged whenever a theatre desperately needs a sure-fire attraction. When performed in entirety *Chūshingura* lasts about eleven hours, but more commonly one or two acts are performed on a given occasion. Indeed, it is relatively rare for any of the famous eighteenth-century plays to be presented except in extracts ranging from a single scene to an act or two. Because these works were originally composed as a series of scenes, no great violence is done to the text if only one episode is presented, though the same would hardly be true of a more highly organized play; the sleepwalking scene from *Macbeth* would not make much sense to an audience unfamiliar with the rest of the play. The Bunraku audiences today usually prefer a set of scenes from five different plays to a single complete work, enjoying the highlights, marked usually by such non-literary devices as a chanter's prolonged hysterical laugh or violent weeping and sobbing, or a striking sequence of poses by the puppets.

The disproportionate importance of such non-literary elements did not lessen in any way the dependence of Bunraku on the texts. A prodigal outpouring of new puppet plays by many writers attracted audiences, eager for novelty, to Bunraku, and Kabuki could do no better than follow its lead. Eventually, however, the flood of talent subsided, and with the death of Chikamatsu Hanji (1725–1783), Bunraku lost its last great author. Once playwrights deserted Bunraku for Kabuki, its days of prosperity were ended. The last decades of the eighteenth century saw the closing of the Takemoto and Toyotake theatres, the two pillars of Bunraku whose competition had fostered so much progress. Only small theatres scattered in various parts of Osaka preserved the texts and traditions.

THE NINETEENTH CENTURY AND AFTERWARDS

At this dark moment in *jōruri* history, a puppeteer from the island of Awaji named Masai Kahei, but familiarly known by his stage name of Bunrakken (or Bunraku-ken), performed with his troupe and scored something of a success. He decided to start a club for amateurs of the art, and after a time had gathered enough talent around him to form a local company. A small theatre was established inside the precincts of the Inari Shrine in Osaka where, under the name of "Bunrakken's Company," it staged puppet plays. Despite many vicissitudes, some occasioned by the drastic governmental reform of the theatre in 1842, Bunrakken's Company not only established itself as the outstanding puppet troupe in Osaka, but eventually in 1872, with the opening of the Bunraku Theatre, the name Bunraku itself came to be used as the general name for the Osaka variety of orthodox puppet entertainments.

The Meiji period (1868–1912) marked a sharp revival of interest in Bunraku, and the names of the great chanters, puppet operators, and samisen players of that time are now almost legends. Most celebrated of all was the samisen player Toyozawa Dampei (1827–1898), a man fanatically devoted to his art, whose influence extended to every aspect of Bunraku. Not only did Dampei's phenomenal skill win for the samisen an esteem it had never before enjoyed in the puppet theatre, but under his merciless tutelage several chanters became masters, and puppet operators were inspired to new heights. Dampei himself composed new plays and scores, including "The Miracle at Tsubosaka Temple" (*Tsubosaka Reigen-ki*) (written with the collaboration of his wife), the most recent *jōruri* to gain a firm place in the repertory. In 1884, when a new Bunraku theatre was founded at the Goryō Shrine, Dampei left the company over a disagreement, and joined the newly founded Hikoroku Theatre. His participation in the new company initiated a period of strenuous rivalry between the two theatres reminiscent of that between the Takemoto and Toyotake Theatres over a hundred years before, and resulting eventually in the attainment of the highest standards of performance since that time. The outstanding puppeteer, Yoshida Tamazō (1829–1905), is today ranked with Tatsumatsu Hachirobei and Yoshida Bunzaburō, masters of Chikamatsu's day, as one of the three supreme puppet operators of Bunraku history, and the combination of Dampei, Tamazō, and the powerful chanter Nagatodayū approached perfection. Dampei died of a cerebral hemorrhage during the course of a performance while playing at the Inari Theatre, the successor to the Hikoroku Theatre.

Despite the general prosperity of the Bunraku Theatre during the Meiji period, its affairs were badly managed by Bunrakken's descendants, and in 1909 the theatre and its assets were sold to the Shōchiku Company. The troupe at the time the management changed included thirty-eight chanters, fifty-one samisen players, and twenty-four puppet operators. *Jōruri* recitations enjoyed a considerable vogue during the late Meiji era, thanks mainly to attractive women chanters who accompanied themselves as they sang and recited the plays, but the Bunraku Theatre itself seemed clearly on the downgrade.

A disastrous fire in 1926 destroyed the Bunraku Theatre together with most of the valuable old puppet heads, treasures which could never be replaced. Re-establishing Bunraku entailed serious financial problems for the owners, and not until the end of 1929 was a new theatre made available. In the meanwhile, the Bunraku company had traveled widely in Japan, notably to Tokyo, creating a new popularity in that city, where puppet plays had not enjoyed much favor since the seventeenth century. The company included splendid artists in all three branches, the most famous of whom were Toyotake Kōtsubodayū (born 1878, later known as Yamashiro-no-shōjō), Yoshida Bungorō (1869-1962, later known as Naniwa-no-jō) and Yoshida Eiza (1872–1945). Kōtsubodayū, a marvelously expressive chanter, was renowned especially for the psychological understanding he displayed of the major works, a quality which set him apart from the famous chanters of the previous generation, who owed their fame to their sweet voices or ringing tones or echoing laughs rather than to any depth of understanding. To watch Kōtsubodayū recite a part was in itself a theatrical experience which needed no puppets. The leading puppeteers (notably Bungorō and Eiza) were no less skillful in their art, both being known for their interpretations of the female roles. Such artists would in the past have drawn large audiences to see Bunraku, but hardly had the company settled in its new theatre than, in 1931, the Manchurian War began. Admissions had been disappointing during the previous year, and in the attempt to arouse public interest otherwise absorbed by the war, such patriotic works as "Three Heroes, Glorious Human Bullets" (1932) by Matsui Shōō, dramatizing an incident in the fighting at Shanghai less than two months before, were elaborately staged, with great attention devoted to mechanisms which permitted the puppets taking the parts of soldiers to smoke cigarettes convincingly. The new plays enjoyed some success, but did not alter the basically gloomy prospects for Bunraku. In 1933 the Japanese Diet passed a bill which had as its object the preservation of the Bunraku Theatre by governmental subsidy, underlining the inability of the puppet theatre to draw audiences of the size attending the films or Kabuki. In the same year, the Bunraku Theatre was turned into a newsreel theatre, and for almost a year the company was forced to perform outside Osaka. It was rumored even among the players that Bunraku's days were numbered. The company struggled through the thirties, the members supplementing their meager earnings with outside teaching. During the war years 1941-45 Bunraku enjoyed a temporary resurgence of activity thanks to the government encouragement of "pure" Japanese art, but this period came to a crashing close with the bombing of Osaka and the burning of the Bunraku Theatre in 1945, this time completing the destruction of such treasured old properties as had survived the fire of 1926.

Once the war ended, Bunraku started performance again in 1946 in the hastily rebuilt, dingy theatre at Yotsuhashi. The company was good as ever, but it drew small audiences, and again voices of doom were heard. The institution by the government of the designation "Human Cultural Properties" called the public's attention to the many superlative artists in the company, ushering in another brief period of prosperity. The company moved in 1956 to a new, luxurious theatre on the Dōtombori, its traditional site, and in 1963 was placed under the management of the newly formed Bunraku Association (Bunraku Kyōkai), an organization which superseded the Shōchiku Company in the management of Bunraku, and transferred direction of the theatre to a non-profit organization which included the performers and representatives of the government and the Japan Broadcasting Corporation. New plans were announced for raising the standards of programs, but again a brief flurry of general interest and excitement quickly subsided.

One reason for the loss of a wide public following is that the texts, written in the poetic, artificial language of two hundred years ago, have become difficult to understand. The texts are so intimately associated with the music and the movements of the puppets that it would not be feasible to simplify them; in any case, drastic changes in the familiar words would be resisted by lovers of Bunraku as much as a modernization of Shakespeare would be in England. Not only do the words fail to capture the full attention of most spectators, but Bunraku usually seems extremely slow to people accustomed to the helter-skelter pace of motion pictures. Fundamentally, however, the problem in appreciation of Bunraku today is that the plays belong to a Japan which either no longer exists or is buried so deeply as to be almost undiscoverable. Bunraku attracted large audiences in the eighteenth century because the theatre staged new plays of immediate appeal. It attracted audiences on an equally large scale in the Meiji period, though by that time it had become chiefly a repertory theatre, because Japan and the Japanese had not changed very greatly in the intervening century or so. The young man of 1890 knew from childhood the plots of the famous plays and even snatches of the dialogue. The language, though not his own speech, presented no great difficulties, if only because the popular novels of the day were filled with the same, traditional phrases. And the ideals implied in the plays, certainly not those of the new, enlightened Meiji era, were still perfectly familiar, and the appeal of the situations as strong as ever.

The greatest popular successes, on the whole, belonged to the romantic variety of theatre which depicts actions of which the public imagines itself capable, though unlikely ever to perform, rather than life as it is normally led. Chikamatsu tended to romanticize his characters—surely not *all* prostitutes of his day could have been so self-sacrificing and faithful to their true loves as those portrayed in his plays—but his domestic tragedies were reasonably faithful to the society in which he lived. Most of the plays of the later eighteenth century, on the other hand, even if given a historical setting, evoke a world of fantasy and dream fulfillment. The frequency of scenes of head inspections, of extraordinary self-sacrifice, or of peerless devotion of wives to their husbands reflects actual life less than it expresses how the townspeople, even men and women leading most sedentary, unexciting lives, liked to imagine themselves behaving, much as pharmacists or grocers in the American West today feel a sense of identification with the heroes of films about frontier days. The man who could not possibly suppose that he would ever have to behead his own son in order to save his master's child nevertheless liked to think himself potentially capable of the deed; he was convinced that though killing one's own child was an indescribably painful act, it was amply rewarded by the joy of securing the safety and happiness of one's master.

Modern critics of the "feudal mentality" expressed in these plays usually fail to distinguish between the anger which such subservience arouses in themselves and the sense of gratification which men of the past felt at the thought they had well served their masters. A masterless samurai (a *rōnin*) or a merchant with no master to serve felt less a sense of proud independence than of deprivation. Though no man in his right mind would wish to kill his own son or inspect his brother's severed head, the man who had no chance in his life to demonstrate the fund of loyalty dormant within him found satisfaction in the Bunraku dramas.

The plays still possess dramatic validity, as anyone who permits himself to surrender to their mood will testify, but it is not surprising that many young Japanese declare that they can understand neither the old-fashioned poetic language of the plays nor their outmoded philosophy. Their attitude is regrettable, but we cannot ignore the fact that Bunraku stopped developing at the end of the eighteenth century. Its existence since then, chiefly as a repertory theatre where beloved old classics are performed, has required an audience familiar in advance with the language and even the plots of works to be presented. It is possible to imagine another kind of audience, similar to that in the West (or Japan) for Italian or German opera, which not only tolerates but relishes unconvincing or even ludicrous texts and performances, because the medium itself offers so many compensating beauties. As yet, however, despite efforts to interest students in Bunraku by offering performances at greatly reduced prices, this new kind of audience has not materialized.

In other attempts to attract new customers Bunraku has staged various new works, ranging from adaptations of *Hamlet* and *Madame Butterfly* to modern Japanese tales about a faithful dog, or about a poor half-Negro child, left in the wake of the American occupation, who is mocked by his Japanese classmates for his dark skin, and who finally stands in the snow (until he freezes to death) so that his skin will at last turn white. With the exception of Bunraku adaptation of familiar Nō or Kabuki plays, however, no work composed in the twentieth century has established itself in the repertory.

The collapse of Bunraku has frequently been predicted, but this seems unlikely today in view of the extensive governmental support. A more serious danger is that younger performers, unwilling to put up with the rigorous training which novices accepted in the past as a matter of course, will lower the standards of performance, and that the new audiences, unable to distinguish between mediocre and great artists, will complacently accept the deterioration of standards. But this gloomy shape of things to come is by no means certain. A new generation, bored with the vulgar absurdities of the films and television, may discover that behind the seemingly outdated Bunraku plots, genuine human emotions are expressed in magical language, and that the presentation, unlike the hastily contrived popular entertainments of our day, is artistically conceived and executed to the last detail. If this discovery takes place in time, we may witness in the near future at least a silver age of this unique art.

III. THE TEXTS AND THE CHANTERS

LONG BEFORE the end of the sixteenth century, when the original tale of Princess Jōruri was first shaped into the text of a puppet drama, the Nō theatre had achieved a high degree of literary and dramatic distinction. Its history could be traced back many years, and though its origins had certainly been humble, it was granted the protection of the shoguns in the late fourteenth century, and was subsequently recognized as an important and even indispensable adjunct of court life. The texts of the Nō plays, dating mainly from the early fifteenth century, were carefully preserved in beautifully inscribed Books, and were studied by the nobles, some of whom appeared in private performances given for their own pleasure. Commoners had relatively few opportunities to witness performances of Nō by master actors, but the stories of the plays and the famous passages in the texts were widely known.

It is not surprising, in view of the respect that Nō commanded, that it should have influenced the nascent art of Bunraku, but fundamentally the two arts are so different that the great scholar Watsuji Tetsurō concluded *jōruri* is best understood as a negation of the aesthetic principles of Nō. He contrasted the poetic understatement and powers of suggestion of Nō with the bright coloring and sometimes overblown rhetoric of the *jōruri* texts, comparing the former to the monochrome washes of Muromachi painting and the latter to the polychrome brilliance of the late sixteenth-century screens. Nō, like the monochrome landscapes or the tea ceremony, was guided in its manner of expression by Zen Buddhism, and in the attempt to express ultimate reality tended to ignore or neglect literal truth. The gestures of the Nō actor in time became so stylized that an uninformed spectator could not guess their meaning, though the connoisseur recognized in them indications of an imprecisely but acutely sensed world beyond the visible actions on the stage. The Nō actor playing the part of the blind beggar Yoroboshi must suggest the world of darkness in which he wanders but also the inner light that guides him. The actor's movements are schematized as if in negation of natural walking or gesturing, but in this manner he can suggest in terms at once pure and profound the essential nature of his condition, as the painter of a monochrome landscape using swift, seemingly arbitrary black lines may convey more successfully than a master of color the essence of a landscape. The symbolic, unspoken beauty of the Nō plays was strengthened by the absence of scenery, except for the pine painted on the back wall, by the use of props which are no more than evocative outlines of real objects, and by the musical accompaniment, which serves to punctuate the silence and order it, rather than to please by its melodies.

In Bunraku, on the other hand, thoughts and emotions are not only outwardly expressed but pushed to the limits of exaggeration. The Nō actor indicates that he is weeping by touching his sleeve to his forehead, but the Bunraku chanter may deliver instead a five minute crescendo of sobs and gasps. Like a Momoyama screen painting which depicts cherry blossoms in relief, larger than life, Bunraku attempts to achieve truth in its portrayals by expanding ineffectual or inadequately expressed thoughts and emotions to their full natural implications. Chikamatsu once stated his belief that bluntly saying "How sad!" about an unfortunate happening killed all possibility of evocative expression. He felt that the *jōruri* playwright should be able to convince the audience of the pathos or joy in a situation without characterizing it with the most obvious adjective. His opinion was exceptionally astute, but when we examine his plays, even those ranked as master-pieces, we discover immediately numerous examples of the most unambiguous characterization of emotions. Chikamatsu's relative restraint becomes apparent only when we compare his texts with those of his predecessors. As he himself realized, a *jōruri* play must be filled with exaggerated movement and vitality if life is to be imparted to the wooden puppets. In case of conflict between dramatic and purely literary interest, *jōruri*, unlike Nō, invariably chose the former.

The puppet theatre imposed many demands on its playwrights. The Nō actor consciously attempts to remove human mannerisms from his movements; the puppet operator desires above all that the non-human figure in his hands will display unmistakably human gestures. The *jōruri* text must therefore assist the puppet operator by providing intensely "human" situations. In Nō, any suggestion of lovemaking on the stage, even the barest intimation of a caress, would be unthinkable. To avoid the possibility that the element of romance will introduce an undesirable human touch, the part of the martial hero Yoshitsune is taken by a small boy in plays which concern Yoshitsune and the beautiful Shizuka. In *jōruri* texts, on the other hand, romance is essential, along with such other typically human actions as gross violence, low clowning, and demonstrations of physical prowess, all rejected by the Nō theatre.

If the *jōruri* is correctly interpreted as a reaction to the aristocratic, ritualized symbolism of Nō, we should expect it to be popular, free in its expression, and direct. These qualities are all present, though if we compare *jōruri* to twentieth-century drama instead of to Nō, it may seem of almost aristocratic distinction. The closest parallel, though clearly not an exact one, between *jōruri* and the drama in the West is the Elizabethan theatre. Both stages catered alike to gentry and ground-lings; *jōruri* pleased the former by the novelty of its plots and the flights of beautiful language, and the latter by the mixture of adventure, lachrymose scenes, and low comedy. The main basis of support for *jōruri* came from the commoners, including illiterate farmers who flocked to village performances when the troupes went on tour. The popularity of puppet plays lingers today in remote rural areas, especially on the islands of Sado and Awaji. Originally, the lower classes may have attended *jōruri* rather than Kabuki because the tickets were cheaper, but from the first, despite the imperial patronage it enjoyed, Bunraku was considered a humbler variety of entertainment than Kabuki, which maintained glamorous connections with the gay quarters. The Bunraku dramatists, rather like their counterparts in Elizabethan England, imposed their literary genius on audiences which might have been satisfied with less adorned entertainment, and thereby created a repertory which has survived to this day.

We can easily imagine why audiences, whether aristocratic or plebeian, responded so eagerly to the *jōruri*. However crude the early texts may have been, they were the first full-length dramas performed in Japan. A Nō program consisted of separate one-act plays divided by comical sketches, but a *jōruri* program was usually devoted to one play which related a single, continuous story. *Jōruri* presentations, unlike Nō, made increasing use of settings, props and stage machinery. The musical accompaniment, unlike the austere, staccato drums of Nō, was lively and sometimes erotic, and the combination of declaimed passages (in which the chanter realistically imitated the voices of the characters) and sung passages of greater lyrical beauty, provided an enjoyable variety, keeping the narration even of long monologues from becoming tedious.

Most importantly, the *jōruri* approached drama in the European sense, stressing the conflict between characters and the violent actions which Nō conspicuously avoided. It is true that even in Chikamatsu's works *jōruri* retains such elements of the storyteller's art as descriptions of the scene by the chanter, but his characters possess a dramatic autonomy which contrasts with the vaguely defined personages in Nō, who sometimes speak for themselves, sometimes describe their actions as if seen by an outsider, and at still other times have their own dialogue pronounced for them by the chorus. The ancient heroes depicted in the Nō plays are often deprived of the very attributes which occasioned the original legends about them except for the one trait deemed essential by the dramatist. *Jōruri*, on the other hand, can describe characters in novelistic detail without impairing the dramatic effect. The early *jōruri* and *sekkyō-bushi* (Buddhist morality plays) attempted to engross audiences with their stories rather than to suggest the symbolic world of Nō. The result was inevitably a diminution of the poetry, but it brought a truly theatrical quality to the Japanese drama.

The clearest way to illustrate the new elements found in the *jōruri* texts is to give an example of a typical work. One of the most famous early *jōruri* was *Amida no Munewari* ("The Chest-Splitting of Amida"), performed in 1614 before the Retired Emperor Goyōzei, apparently the first instance of a puppet play having been staged before a palace audience. The courtiers, accustomed to the language and content of the Nō plays, may initially have smiled at the crudity of "The Chest-Splitting of Amida," a work virtually devoid of aristocratic pretensions, but the very unfamiliarity undoubtedly pleased spectators bored with the oft-repeated Nō plays. As so often in Japanese literary or theatrical history, the nobles were ready to welcome a provincial or popular entertainment, whether Nō in its primitive stage or a new kind of verse-making, but generally they attempted before long to modify this novelty to better suit their own tastes. "The Chest-Splitting of Amida," by its very crudity, may have moved an otherwise sophisticated audience into a kind of religious ecstasy, as Watsuji has suggested.

"The Chest-Splitting of Amida," though ostensibly set in India, is Japanese in conception and in all details. The work is in six acts, in keeping with early *jōruri* usage.

The first act describes a rich man who owns seven treasures, including demon-quelling swords and a pine tree which restores youth. Most of all, however, he prizes his two children, a girl of seven and a boy of five. One day the man says to his wife, "Other people worry about the future life because they expect to meet the bodhisattva Miroku when he appears in this world. But we can always make ourselves young again, whenever we like, with our pine. There is no need for us to pray for the future life because we will never die. Why shouldn't we enjoy ourselves by doing wicked things instead of good deeds, for a change?" The wife is easily persuaded, and the couple thereupon devote themselves to doing the opposite of whatever people consider to be good; they burn Buddhist temples, refuse alms to the priests, envy other people's good fortune, and delight in evil. Shakyamuni Buddha, disturbed by the baleful influence of the rich couple on other people, decides to make them cease their wicked ways. He asks the devil kings' help, but when they visit the rich man's house he wards them off with a magic sword. Buddha then sends a multitude of gods of pestilence to afflict the couple but the sword repels them too. Buddha is now absolutely determined to make the rich man suffer. He assembles all his disciples and commands them to fetch the devils of hell. They eagerly comply and return immediately with some three hundred who undertake Buddha's orders. The devils succeed in outwitting the rich man by melting his magic sword with fire. In the end, the man's treasures are destroyed, his servants killed, and molten iron is poured down the throats of the once arrogant couple. Buddha, however, orders the devils not to harm the two children.

The second act relates the plight of the two orphans, who wander the streets as penniless beggars, rejected everywhere. The years pass, and it is now the seventh anniversary of their parents' death. The boy, distressed that he and his sister cannot make the customary offerings to their parents' memory, proposes that they sell their flesh "as food for eagles or hawks" and use the money they receive to pay for sutra-readings and the erection of a commemorative stone. The sister agrees, and the children travel to a nearby kingdom where they offer themselves for sale, but in vain. In great dejection they go to the temple of Amida to pray for a buyer. Amida appears that night in their dreams, praises their devotion, and informs them where they will find a rich man willing to purchase their bodies.

In the third act we are told of a potentate with an only son of twelve who has been stricken by a mysterious malady. The father summons the most famous doctor of India, who declares that the boy's sickness can be cured only if the rich man finds a girl born in the same year, the same month, the same day and the same hour, rips the liver from her body, washes it seventy-five times in an elixir of long life, and feeds it to his ailing son. The rich man offers a huge reward for a girl of the right description, but although more than 350 candidates, all girls of twelve, present themselves, none fits the specifications exactly.

In the fourth act the rich man, learning of the brother and sister who have come to his house to offer themselves for sale, addresses the girl and discovers she was born at precisely the same hour as his son. He directs his wife to give the girl whatever she asks on condition that she allow the liver to be torn from her body. But the wife, struck by the girl's remarkable beauty, suspects that she must be the transformation of some god or Buddha, and fears that if the girl is sacrificed, the wrath of Heaven will descend on the family. She attempts (by describing her son's desperate illness) to persuade the girl to sacrifice herself voluntarily. The girl bursts into tears, not out of self-pity, but because she wonders who will look after her brother if she sacrifices herself. The rich man and his wife join in tears of sympathy.

In the fifth act, the climax of the work, the girl agrees to be sacrificed on condition that the rich man build a temple in memory of her parents, and enshrine in it an Amida triptych. The rich man gladly accepts, and in twenty-one days the work is completed. The girl begs the rich man's protection for her brother. He assures her he will consider the boy as his own son. The girl, satisfied, goes to pray before Amida. She declares, "I offer you this temple, built at the cost of my life. I pray that, however heavy my sins, you will save me because of the merit of this act and bring me rebirth on the same lotus with my parents." She reads aloud sections of the Lotus Sutra: the fifth chapter for her father, the sixth chapter for her mother, the seventh chapter for her brother and for those present, the eighth chapter for herself. The brother is bewildered by these events, but to comfort him the girl declares that she is to become the rich man's bride. She urges the boy to take orders as a monk so that he may pray for their parents' repose. He consents, and exhausted by emotion falls asleep, his head on his sister's lap. She recalls how inseparable they have been through the years and, as she combs his disheveled hair, she remembers that never has a day passed but that she has arranged his hair at least three times. "After tomorrow who will be a sister to him and bind his hair? How sad this is!"

The sixth and final act describes the girl's last day. The rich man's son has become desperately ill, and no further delay is possible. The desperate father sends five soldiers to the temple where the girl is staying, with orders to rip out her liver. They go, but cannot bring themselves to kill so beautiful a girl. She insists and even directs them as to what they must do. In the end they cut open her chest and remove the liver. The rich man has it washed seventy-five times in the elixir of long life, as the doctor prescribed, and feeds it to his son, who at once perceptibly improves. By that night, the boy having recovered completely, his overjoyed attendants go to examine the dead girl's body. They discover her and her brother sleeping peacefully, hand in hand. Beside them the statue of Amida Buddha is streaming with blood from a terrible rent in its chest, and it is apparent to all that Amida has offered his own liver to save the girl. The rich man decides on the spot that the girl will be his son's bride. The brother, as he previously agreed, will become a priest. People gather from everywhere to pay homage before the mutilated, blood-stained statue of Amida Buddha.

"The Chest-Splitting of Amida" has been described in detail because it differs so conspicuously from either the Nō dramas or the stories about Princess Jōruri, based as they were on familiar materials and couched in traditional language. The play is noteworthy also for the many themes which were to figure prominently in the later puppet theatre. Watsuji Tetsurō, noting that the first mentions of "The Chest-Splitting of Amida" date from about 1614, when major edicts by the government aimed at the prohibition of Christianity were promulgated, has suggested that Christian influence may account for certain curiously untraditional aspects of the plot. In the first act, for example, Shakyamuni Buddha, not at all resembling the all-compassionate deity described in other Buddhist works, is filled with divine wrath at the arrogance of the rich man who fears nothing from the world after death, and sends avenging devils to torment the man, who is finally stripped of his vaunted treasures. The story is reminiscent of Job's, and the Shakyamuni here is more like Jehovah than Buddha. The Amida Buddha of the final act, however, suggests Christ; nothing in previous Japanese depictions of Amida accounts for the scene of people worshiping a holy image streaming with blood, in the manner of European (and especially Iberian) representations of Christ on the cross. Amida's sacrifice of himself to save the girl also suggests Christ's offering himself to save mankind. It is impossible to prove the existence of direct influence, but one can surely recognize an enormous difference between the deity here described and the traditional portrayals of Amida in his remote Western Paradise. Christian art and even stories from the Bible were well enough known to some Japanese at the time to account for this unconventional Amida.

The theme of substitution, stated in "The Chest-Splitting of Amida" in such extreme terms, was to be a most familiar feature of *jōruri* texts. In Chikamatsu's first great success, "Kagekiyo Victorious" (*Shusse Kagekiyo*, 1685), the final scene is largely devoted to a description of the miracle by which Kannon, the special object of Kagekiyo's devotion, saves him from execution by substituting her head for his; the bloodstained, decapitated image of Kannon is discovered after Kagekiyo had presumably been beheaded, much as in the play about Amida. Substitutions of one person to save another may be found in earlier Japanese literature and need not have derived from Christian sources or even from "The Chest-Splitting of Amida," but its prominence as a theme probably owes much to this early *jōruri* success.

Other themes in this play which would frequently reappear include the sufferings of innocent children whose devotion to the memory of their parents is finally rewarded, and the use of some extraordinary medicine to work a seemingly impossible cure. One might mention especially "Gappō's Daughter Tsuji" (*Sesshū Gappō ga Tsuji*, 1773), in which the young Shuntoku, suffering from leprosy, is cured by drinking blood from the liver of a woman born in the hour of the tiger, the day of the tiger, the month of the tiger and the year of the tiger, obviously an echo of the Amida play written over 150 years before.

"The Chest-Splitting of Amida," it needs hardly be said, bears no resemblance to the condensed, intricate structure of a Nō play, either in plot or language. Its ancestry, apart from possible foreign influence, is to be found in the popular stories composed in the Muromachi period about the miracles of the gods and Buddhas. The diction is simple and rarely poetic, and there is no attempt to suggest any profounder truths than the story so straightforwardly told. It is superior to the Nō in purely dramatic terms, if only because it contains a variety of characters, and is not focused exclusively on one central figure. The play is interesting otherwise because, unlike the original "Tale in Twelve Episodes" it appears to have been composed from the start as a puppet play. The scene in which the soldiers tear the liver from the girl's body, for example, could be performed realistically, thanks to the use of puppets. At the same time, in more artistic terms, it was possible to assign the major roles to children; in a theatre of actors one may not be able to find a twelve-year-old who can read convincingly a series of passages from the Lotus Sutra, but in the puppet theatre where all parts are delivered by the chanters, a child puppet can be entrusted with the most difficult roles. Certainly one difference between the Japanese and European theatre of the seventeenth and eighteenth centuries is the prominence of children in the former.

The contrast with the Nō must have been welcomed by the blasé aristocrats, and some may not only have patronized the *jōruri* but written texts as well, sensing its as yet scarcely explored literary and dramatic possibilities. But most advances in the artistic techniques of *jōruri*, whatever contributions the nobility may have made, are closely connected with the successive famous chanters, each of whom strongly impressed his personality on the art.

The chanters have been at once the servants and creators of the texts. In the Kabuki theatre, where the actors always remained the center of attention, the playwright wrote his texts to fit the special talents of a particular actor, who felt free to alter the text in any way he chose. Even Chikamatsu had to yield to this convention, though unwillingly; it is often suggested that he turned from Kabuki to Bunraku because of his irritation at the liberties the Kabuki actors took with his texts. The Kabuki text tended to be no more than a vehicle for the histrionic talents of the actors. Chikamatsu himself on occasion left the climactic scene of a play a mere outline, knowing actors would prefer to improvise their lines. In Bunraku, on the other hand, the chanters are bound to the text, which they have before them throughout the performances though they know every word by heart. They could not make radical departures from the text even if they so chose without considerable advance preparation, for the movements of the puppets and the samisen accompaniment must correspond exactly to the text; if the chanters improvised like Kabuki actors the effect would be disastrous. Even the prolongation of a syllable becomes in Bunraku a major change, establishing a new tradition of reading a part; the second Tsunadayū, when chanting Hambei's confession from the "Saké Shop" scene in 1822, added a cough which has since become traditional among chanters who bear the name Tsunadayū.

Although the chanters are far more closely bound to the text than Kabuki actors, even in the same parts, they have inspired and even created the styles of the *jōruri* playwrights. When the chanter Uji Kaga-no-jō (1635-1711), known for his musical talents and his fondness for the Nō plays, expressed preference for more melodious and elegant works, the *jōruri* playwrights met his requirements, much as Kabuki playwrights provided the first Ichikawa Danjūrō with opportunities to dazzle the audiences with his "roughhouse" *(aragoto)* antics, or the romantic Sakata Tōjūrō with his tender love scenes *(wagoto)*. Chikamatsu wrote *Yotsugi Soga* ("The Soga Heir"), perhaps his maiden work, for Kaga-no-jō in 1683, and the chanter's influence is apparent in the work. Earlier plays about the Soga brothers had emphasized their bold deeds, but in this work attention is shifted from the heroic brothers to the courtesans Tora and Shōshō. Not only did this create a more sophisticated atmosphere, the demi-monde so familiar in Chikamatsu's later works, but it provided room for displaying Kaga-no-jō's voice to best advantage. The Kyoto audiences, which had never taken to the Edo-style heroics, were delighted, and the triumph was shared equally by Kaga-no-jō and Chikamatsu. Later, when Chikamatsu composed texts for Gidayū, he gave his historical plays a tragic depth such works had previously lacked. Gidayū's peculiar talents inspired Chikamatsu to compose the first domestic tragedies, the two men apparently collaborating closely. After Gidayū's death, Chikamatsu again changed his style, this time to accord with the less powerful delivery of Masadayū, the youthful successor of Gidayū. The proportion of domestic tragedies to Chikamatsu's entire output of plays dropped markedly, presumably again in response to the chanter's demands. The composition of the texts indeed was so closely related to the chanters that for the period of *jōruri* before Chikamatsu the texts are known by the names not of the playwrights but of the chanters, and even today the authors' names are often omitted from the playbills.

The chanters have always been considered the intellectuals and even the gentlemen of Bunraku. The outstanding chanter Takemoto Tsunadayū, to cite one instance, was an accomplished scholar of *jōruri* texts, though some puppet operators are virtually illiterate. By its very nature, of course, the chanter's work involves not only imitation of his predecessors, equally true of puppet operators and samisen players, but continual study of the texts. When neglected plays are revived the chanter is often obliged to interpret the parts afresh, for the notations in the old texts are generally too crude to be of much service. Of course, it is desirable in such cases to find someone with knowledge of the old traditions. In 1920, for example, Tsunadayū discovered that the wife of a Bunraku scholar had learned as a child from an elderly samisen player the traditional delivery of Chikamatsu's play *Kasane-izutsu*, a work which had not been performed since 1877. Tsunadayū studied the play with her, but not until 1952 did he have the opportunity of reciting the part at the Bunraku Theatre, where it was revived after a lapse of seventy-seven years. Tsunadayū, having once learned the traditions, was able to recall them thirty-two years later, a feat of memory not considered exceptional in a chanter.

A beautiful voice is of course a great asset to a chanter, but even if his voice is weak or (like Gidayū's) a metallic rasp, he may still reach the heights of his profession by the effectiveness of his interpretation and recitation of the texts. He need not possess an actor's looks, but he must be equipped with the stamina to throw himself completely into as long as a full hour's impassioned solo delivery. In the past, chanters normally were the sons (real or adopted) of other chanters, and men who attempted to enter the profession from the outside were looked upon with suspicion and even contempt. This attitude stems from the belief that only someone familiar with the sounds of *jōruri* and its traditions from earliest childhood could hope to master them. The great Toyotake Kōtsubodayū (born in 1878), honored by the court in 1947 with the title of Yamashiro-no-shōjō, suffered in his early career from the disadvantage of having been born in Tokyo and not in Osaka, the home of Bunraku. Even today this feeling has not entirely disappeared, though an artist like Kōtsubodayū eventually can overcome such prejudices by his undeniable skill.

Tsunadayū, Kōtsubodayū's successor, began his career in Bunraku very early. He was first taken to the theatre by his father, a Bunraku enthusiast, at the age of four or five, and began his study of chanting with a teacher in the neighborhood shortly afterwards. On August 15, 1911, at the age of seven, he was formally accepted as a pupil by Kōtsubodayū, who bestowed on the boy the name Toyotake Tsubamedayū, a name he himself had used early in his career. In Bunraku, as in Kabuki, the names of great performers are preserved by transmitting them from one generation to the next. These names all have rankings and special traditions. The name Tsunadayū, for example, was one within Kōtsubodayū's power to bestow. As early as 1941 he felt that Tsubamedayū was ready for the honor of assuming the name of the eighth Tsunadayū, but his pupil was reluctant to accept this honor, and took instead a lesser name, the sixth Orinodayū, an early name used by the sixth Tsunadayū. Not until 1947, when Kōtsubodayū received his court title, did his pupil finally succeed as the eighth Tsunadayū.

He had demonstrated his right to this honor by distinguishing himself at each of the prescribed stages in a chanter's career. His performing career began at the age of thirteen in 1917 with a minor part, barely half a page long, in the middle section of the opening act of *Chūshingura*. He moved next to chanting the beginning and middle sections of the conclusion of first acts, then to the beginning and middle sections of the second act, and finally to the beginning of the third act, a vital stage in a chanter's career. At this level the chanter may progress either to the conclusion of the first act, or to the middle of the third act, both considered extremely demanding. The concluding section of an act carries the most prestige for a chanter; in Kōtsubodayū's words, "The first time a chanter sees the notation 'conclusion' beside his name in the program, he feels like a university graduate looking at his diploma." However, the conclusion of the second act, technically ranked as a section of major importance, tends to be dull and is therefore generally assigned to unpopular though senior chanters. Tsunadayū relates that he enjoyed especially performing the beginning of the fourth act, not only because of the opportunities it offered to display his talents, but because it was usually performed just after lunch, and the audience was likely to be larger and more attentive than when hungry.

The third and fourth acts are the high points of the performance, and the chanter is allowed to deliver these sections only after he has fully demonstrated his proficiency. Normally an attempt is made to assign chanters congenial roles, but often the best roles have been pre-empted by a senior performer, and only when he falls ill or retires can the younger chanter, however proficient, hope to assume them. Substitution at the last moment for an ailing star is the dream of all Bunraku artists, for it offers the one opportunity of advancing more quickly than by mere seniority. Tsunadayū was called upon to substitute for his teacher Kōtsubodayū on several important occasions, and so distinguished himself each time that as a reward he was assigned roles normally taken by much senior men. Needless to say, such proficiency was the product of his intense study both of the performances of his teacher (and other great chanters) and of the texts. Tsunadayū amusingly related how, when he learned he was to substitute for his teacher in reciting "Gappo's Daughter Tsuji," one of the most difficult plays of the repertory, he gorged himself on steaks, eels, and every other variety of especially nourishing food in order to fortify himself for the ordeal.

Many stories describe how chanters struggled to improve their art. A famous anecdote tells of the chanter who perfected a heroic laugh by delivering it from successively higher floors of the seven-storied pagoda of the Tennōji, demanding each time of a friend on its ground if it could clearly be heard. Even if he does not resort to such expedients, the chanter's training is highly demanding. Apart from learning how to render the texts, the young chanter must be familiar with the traditional etiquette expected in his relations with his teacher and other seniors. It is a disciple's duty, for example, to offer his teacher tea at pauses in the narration; it has been claimed that a pupil who knows how to serve tea properly himself ranks as a full-fledged artist. This means that the pupil must be so sensitive to the master's voice that he will be aware instantly of any departures from its usual standards, and will know whether ground ginger or a raw egg in the tea would best alleviate the particular vocal defect. Moreover, he must not wait for the master's cup to be emptied before he fills it again, nor should he allow the tea to grow cold. In the dressing room the young Bunraku performer must show his awareness of his humble position by wearing only cotton kimonos. The pupil, whether in the dressing room or a private place, may not sit on a cushion in his teacher's presence; Tsunadayū recalled that only after Kōtsubodayū retired did he at last comply with the suggestion that he sit on a cushion, though even then with great hesitation and feelings of impropriety. Such deference was considered essential in the past, and remains the general practice today. Some artists have rebelled at the old system—Tsunadayū himself, in disgust at the rarity of opportunities given him to perform important roles, for five years (from 1936 to 1941) elected to perform *jōruri* without puppets as a member of a small company of similarly-minded younger artists. Again, after the end of the war, when a Bunraku union was formed, most of the senior performers, including the chanter Toyotake Kōtsubodayū, the puppet operator Yoshida Bungorō and the samisen player Tsurusawa Seiroku, refused to join, believing that it was improper for artists to bicker about money. "As long as you have the chance to show your talent, people won't forget you," Kōtsubodayū told his pupil. At first Tsunadayū, who belonged to a younger generation less governed by such traditional views, took the side of those who had formed the union, but the ties of master and disciple proved too strong, and before long he rejoined Kōtsubodayū. The company, however, remained divided, the break not being formally mended until 1963 with the formation of the Bunraku Association. In the meanwhile, the chanters had continued to perform their task of training their successors. On August 15, 1953, exactly forty-four years after his father, Tsunadayū's son was accepted as a pupil by Yamashiro-no-shōjō and given the name of Tsunakodayū. Despite the gloom of some prophets, the traditions of the chanter's art seem in no immediate danger of perishing.

IV. THE SAMISEN AND THE PLAYERS

THE SAMISEN (or shamisen) is by far the most popular Japanese musical instrument. In the smallest of its three common sizes it is an indispensable element in geisha entertainments, the old-fashioned boating party, or the folk festival. It serves also as the accompaniment for a large variety of ballads ranging from brief love-songs to long, painfully narrated monologues about the chivalrous gamblers of a century ago. In the Kabuki theatre it provides the basic melodic background for the *nagauta* and other types of narrative singing. The middle size of samisen is used in the style of narration called Tokiwazu and in *jiuta*, an instrumental ensemble which often accompanies dancing. The largest samisens, considerably heavier than the *nagauta* variety and played with a plectrum almost twice as big, are employed exclusively in *jōruri* performances, where strong and incisive notes, rather than melodious or poetic tones, are required. Paul Claudel once likened the sound of the *jōruri* samisen to that of a nerve being plucked.

Whatever the size of the samisen or the manner of playing, it is primarily an accompaniment to the voice, and not a solo instrument. It is tuned to no fixed basic pitch, but can be modulated at will to blend with the voice of the singer. The samisen consists of three main elements: the body, the neck, and the handle. The materials used to make each part have been tested and improved over the centuries, and are now carefully ranked in order of desirability. For the body of the instrument Chinese quince is preferred, followed by mulberry wood; cherry wood is considered a poor substitute. The neck and handle are preferably of *kōki* wood, followed by red sandalwood, then by oak or cherry wood. The tuning pegs in the handle are of black sandalwood or ivory. The kind of skin used to cover the box, the materials for the three strings, the bridge, the plectrum, and all the other parts of the samisen have been studied with infinite care, and the proportions and shape of the instrument have been subjected to many changes. Such attention to improving the samisen, an instrument associated with the world of pleasure rather than with the noble Confucian art of music, suggests its peculiar appeal to the Japanese, as well as the awareness of successive generations of musicians of precisely the kind of sounds they desired. The music of the samisen employed in *jōruri* is not nearly so ingratiating as the *nagauta* samisen, but this is no accident or fault of the musicians; in Bunraku the samisen's function is to enhance the chanter's recitation and to guide the puppet operators in their movements. Opportunities for exhibiting virtuoso musicianship exist, but they are of only secondary importance.

The exact methods of tuning and playing the samisen are rather beyond the scope of a general essay such as this. Even though the non-musician who attends a Bunraku play may be uninformed about these technical matters, he cannot escape becoming aware of the samisen's decisive role in a performance. When, at the beginning of a scene, the turntable on the dais to the right of the stage revolves and brings before the audience a chanter and a samisen player, it will almost certainly prove to be a combination so perfectly matched that it is hard to distinguish the part of each man in the total effect. Takemoto Tsunadayū, for example, was accompanied for more than twenty-five years by Takezawa Yashichi, and the two men formed so sensitive a partnership that Yashichi could tell intuitively, almost from Tsunadayū's first phrase, how his performance would go that day. If he sensed that Tsunadayū was in his best form, he would feel free to vary the tempos in order to afford Tsunadayū maximum opportunities for virtuoso display, but if, on the other hand, he judged that Tsunadayū's performance would be slow in reaching its normal level, or that he was having an off-day altogether, he would adjust his playing accordingly to cover the deficiencies. The inarticulate cries with which the samisen player punctuates his performance may help the chanter when he himself is in difficulty, but if he is in good voice he is likely to resent these interruptions which divert attention from himself. When a combination of chanter and samisen as well-matched as Tsunadayū perform, the samisen player may not utter a single *hah* or *oh* all evening, but usually the beginning of a new scene, particularly the *michiyuki*, or a change in atmosphere within a given scene, will elicit a sharp cry from the samisen player. Some players indulge ostentatiously in a whole repertory of cries, but this violates the proper functions of an accompaniment, and though welcomed by members of the audience, is essentially the mark of an inferior artist.

The interpretation of the text is usually determined by the chanter, then conveyed to the samisen player, who becomes the conductor of the performance. The chanter cannot sing until he hears the appropriate notes, nor can the puppet operators move out onto the stage. The temptation to be a tyrant exists, but the samisen player usually takes advantage of his position as conductor only so as to impart the flexibility necessary in a performance to keep it from growing stale. The familiar cliché that the samisen player must be a "wife" to the chanter sometimes has an ironic ring; the "wife" may turn out to be a shrew and compel the chanter to act the part of the docile husband. The samisen virtuoso Toyozawa Dampei was famous for having on one occasion repeated so many times a series of notes calling for a certain exclamation from the chanter that the latter collapsed with exhaustion over his stand. Dampei, it should be said, was not indulging in sadistic torment of a fellow artist. He had decided that this particular effect was necessary in terms of the performance as it had progressed that day, and he used his prerogative as leader of the ensemble to impose his artistic conception on the chanter. Dampei was a unique figure, and no samisen player today would repeat his stunt; nevertheless, however unassuming the player may be, his authority is like that of the opera conductor, whose beat must be followed even by the temperamental prima donna if the combination of voices and orchestra is not to be cacophonous. An indecisive or blurred samisen accompaniment can work equal devastation on the manipulation of the puppets if it causes the operators to miss their cues. The player's responsibility is heavy, and the training for his share of a Bunraku performance is accordingly strict.

Samisen players are usually born in the Bunraku milieu; if not, they are likely to have family connections with another school of playing. Lessons begin early for the child who shows an avocation for the samisen. By the time he is seven or eight he may have already demonstrated his proficiency sufficiently to be enrolled as the pupil of an established Bunraku player. Being the pupil of a great performer may in practice mean no more than having unlimited opportunities to hear him play. Actual instruction is given mainly by older pupils, and often this used to consist (if no longer true today) of blows and harsh words, rather than of helpful advice. The justification for such savage treatment was that it served to weed out young people not wholly devoted to their art. The scalp wounds dealt by the master's plectrum were the samisen player's equivalent of the Heidelberg dueling scar.

The young player, to a greater degree even than the fledgling chanter or puppet operator, was constantly kept practicing. One distinguished artist recalled how as a child he had begged for a fire in the bitter-cold rehearsal room. "Very well, I'll see that you get a fire," said his teacher to the overjoyed boy, only to add, "Just as soon as you learn how to play." Rehearsals in the summer were even more arduous. One teacher is reported to have insisted that each pupil keep practicing until a pint of sweat could be wrung from the sheet on which he sat. Such training inevitably drove some young men into other professions, but it also produced masters whose likes may never be heard again.

Today the samisen player at the chanter's left on the revolving dais sits erect in formal Japanese style, his legs tucked under him, but, as we know from old paintings, this was not the original posture for playing the instrument. In the seventeenth century the samisen player sat cross-legged, or on a little chair, or with one knee raised. The posture now considered essential to a good performance originated about 1700 in the licensed quarters of Kyoto and Osaka, and spread then to the theatre. The Bunraku player sits with the base of his samisen resting on his right leg, two to five inches from the kneecap. He holds the instrument at a forty-five degree angle, the handle pointing over his left shoulder. He props the neck of the instrument between the thumb and index finger of his left hand, gripping it with the remaining fingers. A plectrum held in his right hand is used to strike the strings stretched over the body of the samisen.

Forty-eight positions of the left hand on the strings have been distinguished, each designated by a letter of the Japanese syllabary. This system of notation was invented at the end of the eighteenth century by Tsurusawa Seishichi, reportedly a boy of twelve at the time. The player presses one of these forty-eight points with the index finger of his left hand and produces the desired note when the plectrum hits the string. The samisen has two bridges, one at the base of the instrument, and the other in the handle. The lowest of the three strings does not pass over the upper bridge, but reverberates over a cavity in the handle with a sound characteristic of the instrument. Other typical sounds occur when the plectrum strikes the string and the catskin at the same time with a sharp snap, or when the operator slides his left hand down the strings. The range of the first string extends from B below middle C to B above middle C; of the second string from E above middle C to the E one octave higher; and of the third string from B below high C to the B one octave higher.

The musical notation for the samisen indicates the note and its length (normal, double, four times). The length is relative, not measured by a metronome, giving the player a good deal more leeway than in Western music. Notations sometimes indicate the mood (sad, joyous, and so on) produced by the manner of touch and, in the case of the *jōruri* samisen only, describe the chanter's delivery, whether declamation or song, and the pitch and length of his notes. Certain fixed patterns signaling the end of a scene, the entrance and exits of the puppets, and other important moments are also noted in the score.

A performance, whether of a complete play or of only a single scene, invariably begins with a samisen passage which creates the desired mood. In addition to such fairly extended solos, brief motifs serve as shorthand indications of emotions being portrayed. Resignation, for example, is expressed by playing B below middle C on the first string, high C on the third string, and F on the second string; joy by high C followed by high E on the third string; love merely by high C on the third string. Imploration requires seven notes, and confusion twelve. A combination of such patterns runs through the musical accompaniment of the plays, indicative of the samisen's primary function of corroborating the words of the chanter and the gestures of the puppets.

The composition of the music for a puppet play has generally been left to the samisen players. The most demanding part of the task is the composition of the solo passages which give the player his brief moments of glory. In some works five or six samisens play simultaneously to create a colorful and usually cheerful effect, and in the *michiyuki* sections of the plays, popular ballads of the period are introduced, affording additional scope for the player's talents. There are a few traditional feats, reminiscent of the drum major with his baton, which allow the player a rare chance to perform a vaudeville turn. Apart from these infrequent opportunities, the samisen's role is auxiliary, and the music seldom more than the chords accompanying recitative in a European opera.

Certain other instruments besides the samisen are occasionally heard in Bunraku performances. The *koto*, a seven-stringed, zither-like instrument, is featured in several famous scenes, and the *kokyū*, a violin-like instrument played with a bow, sometimes accompanies tragic moments because of its peculiarly doleful sound. Offstage battles are indicated by drums and gongs; and bells, flutes, and other instruments make their appearance when required by the text. The war play "Three Heroes, Glorious Human Bullets," produced in 1932, is remembered today because it introduced the bugle to Bunraku.

V. THE PUPPETS AND THE OPERATORS

Bunraku owes to the puppets, its most distinctive feature, the high reputation it has won at home and abroad. The leading puppeteers enjoy a personal popularity at least as great as that of any chanter or samisen player, and a master like Kiritake Monjūrō could impose his interpretations on a whole performance. We should expect, then, that the operators would be considered no less than the equals of the chanters and samisen players, but the situation has clearly been otherwise. Puppetry and the operators themselves were long subject to denigration, not only on the part of society but as an official policy of the government, which imposed restrictions on the activities of puppet operators that did not apply to chanters or samisen players. Even today the operators tend to be looked down on socially, if only because many are badly educated or given to drink and gambling. Beneath such objections it is also possible to detect traces of the ancient belief, going back to the days of the *kugutsu-mawashi*, that puppet operators were foreigners, unlike other Japanese. In rural areas where primitive varieties of puppet plays are still preserved, the operators are sometimes subjected to open discrimination, and if such attitudes are no longer taken seriously by educated people, they account for an undercurrent of opinion that the chanter and the samisen player rank as artists, but the puppet operator is little better than a skilled workman.

Certainly it is true that the operators' approach to this task differs markedly from the chanters' or samisen players'. He is bound by traditions no less than they, but these traditions are completely unrecorded, and are remembered more by the body than by the mind. If one asks a chanter or samisen player to explain some detail in his performance, he will probably be able to answer convincingly, but the operator, because his memory is physical rather than verbal, may content himself with saying, "There's no particular meaning." Unlike the chanter who interprets the texts and brings out a significance which may not be apparent to the reader, or the samisen player who employs musical means to create the atmosphere he deems appropriate, the operator does not use the puppet to express his own conceptions; he enables it to express its own emotions by imparting the strength of his body. We can forget his presence more easily than a chanter's or a samisen player's because he is hardly more than an extension of the puppet. He should be as impersonal as the electric current which indifferently makes a train run on its tracks or brings us over the radio a performance of *Don Giovanni*.

Strictly speaking, of course, this statement is inaccurate: the operators are more than mere motivating forces. Each man not only moves his body like a tennis player in graceful, almost automatic reactions to a changing situation; he must endeavor to allow the puppet a free and natural expression of feelings. Nevertheless, it is fitting that he disappear and that he be unable to verbalize his actions; an intellectual puppet operator would surely be a grotesque failure. Whatever the original causes for the social inequality among the three branches of Bunraku, anonymity is most desirable in the operator. His seeming lack of artistry (the better the operator, the more the puppet appears to move of its own volition), though made light of by other performers, makes it possible for the inanimate puppets to come to life.

The puppets may be classified in various ways. First of all, a division is possible among the different species: marionettes operated from above by strings, mechanical dolls, puppets held above the operators' heads, small puppets worked on a portable stage, large puppets operated by one man and, finally, the three-man puppet of Bunraku. All these varieties still may be found in rural parts of Japan, sometimes preserved by only a few men. The most advanced puppets in every way are those of the Bunraku troupe in Osaka, together with the somewhat coarser variants used by troupes on the island of Awaji and in Tokushima Prefecture. Most Bunraku puppets are operated by three men, but minor characters (bystanders, soldiers, servants) or animals (foxes, horses, tigers) are operated by one man, rather in the manner of the one-man puppets used in *bunya-bushi*, *sekkyō-bushi* and Noroma, three old types of *jōruri* preserved today mainly on the island of Sado. In the seventeenth and eighteenth centuries marionettes and mechanical dolls sometimes supplemented the normal Bunraku puppets for purposes of special effects, but this practice has now disappeared.

Another traditional way of distinguishing the puppets, particularly the Bunraku varieties, is by the sex and age of the characters, both with respect to the frames used for the bodies and to the heads, the focal points of interest in a performance. The male puppets, much larger and heavier than the female, have frames consisting of a straight piece of wood for the shoulder line and a bamboo hoop for the hips. Between the two is pasted thick paper (or sometimes cloth) to form a back and front. Occasionally, in roles which require the puppet to bare his chest, the upper part of the torso is fashioned in the round of cotton cloth, more or less realistically. As a general principle, however, parts of the body covered by the kimono are not delineated. The puppet's head is inserted into the shoulder board, and the arms and legs suspended from the same board at the padded ends. The male puppets are equipped with a fixed bamboo rod at the right of the hoop which the operator uses as a prop to support the weight. The smaller and simpler female puppets lack the feet, the bamboo rod, and the highly articulated hands and facial features.

The three-man puppet is worked by a principal operator, an operator of the left hand, and an operator of the feet. The principal operator inserts his left hand into the puppet from the back under the *obi*, and his right hand through the opening in the upper part of the puppet's right sleeve. With his left hand he grips the armature which extends down from the puppet's neck, thereby moving the head and (if the head is so equipped) the eyes, eyebrows, and mouth, by strings fastened to flexible whalebone strips. With his right hand he operates the puppet's right hand, using a toggle halfway up the puppet's arm to move the whalebone "springs" in the hands. The operator's left hand also moves the puppet's body, whether in motion across the stage or in agitated breathing as it sits in one spot.

The second operator moves the left hand by means of a stick about fifteen inches long joined to the puppet's arm near the elbow. A stick of this length is necessary because this operator cannot come as close to the puppet as the principal operator, who holds the puppet in his arms. The second operator pulls with his right hand cords attached to a toggle on the manipulating stick. Normally he makes no use of his left hand in moving the puppet.

The third operator works the feet of male puppets, guiding himself by the principal operator's movements. He makes the puppet walk or run, stand or sit, as the text requires. This operator not only must convince the audience that the puppet is actually moving on solid ground, but supply appropriate noises of stamping or running by striking his own feet on the floorboards. Female puppets are not provided with feet unless a role specifically requires them. The operator simulates the motions of legs and feet within the kimono by bunching the hems as the character walks, or by rounding the kimono to suggest knees when the puppet sits. Sometimes use is made of a kind of weighted pillow suspended from the bamboo hoop of the puppet frame to give an additional roundness to the figures of female puppets when they sit. As in the case of male puppets, excited movements onstage are amplified by the operator's stamping his feet.

The operators of the left hand and of the feet are attired completely in black and wear gauzy black hoods over their heads. Originally the principal operators were so attired, in the interests of complete anonymity, but as time went on, they came to rival the Kabuki actors in the care with which they adorned themselves. Today, the principal operators normally perform without a hood and in brightly colored formal costumes, though in plays of a particularly tragic nature, they may wear black, and in new or recently revived works they may also wear a hood. Not only the vanity of the principal operators but public demand to see the faces of the famous operators accounts for their rather excessively conspicuous presence in most plays, a violation of the anonymity which should mark these devoted servants of the puppets.

Traditionally, an operator was expected to spend ten years operating the feet and ten years more operating the left arm before he assumed the principal role. In practice, however, there has been no fixed rule. As in other branches of the art, training begins from childhood. The late Kiritake Monjūrō became a pupil of the late Yoshida Bungorō at the age of eight, and made his first stage appearance at twelve. At fourteen he had already gained recognition as an exceptionally skilled operator of the feet, doubtlessly thanks to the guidance he received from Bungorō, long renowned as a master of this art. The young Monjūrō's greatest joy and satisfaction came when he was chosen at fourteen to operate the feet of the puppet Jihei in the *michiyuki* from "The Love Suicides at Amijima," assisting Bungorō, the principal operator. When Monjūrō first put on foot-high clogs, the mark of the principal operator, at the age of twenty-seven, Bungorō, noticing the young man's panic, himself took over the left hand in order to steady his pupil. On one occasion, as Monjūrō gratefully recalled, Bungorō even manipulated the feet to help his pupil, who had been suddenly deprived of his usual assistant.

Such kindness from his teacher undoubtedly contributed enormously to Monjūrō's remarkable development as a puppet operator. His case, it must be said, was unusual. For the most part the senior operators have not only been extremely loath to give away the secrets of their own excellence as performers, but have demonstrated a brutality towards their assistants far surpassing that of senior chanters or samisen players. Their reluctance to impart systematically to pupils the fruits of their own experience mainly reflects their ignorant fear and jealousy of young talent. The operation of puppets, unlike the recitation of texts or the playing of the samisen, depends not so much on maturity of interpretation as on the acquisition of certain knacks which could be taught fairly easily and which contribute enormously to the total effectiveness of a performance. It may readily be conceived that a man who has spent years painfully mastering these little skills without benefit of guidance would be reluctant to impart them to a pupil in the course of an hour's instruction.

Many of the best operators have been self-taught. The first Yoshida Eiza (1872–1945), considered by critics to have been the most accomplished puppeteer of this century, once explained how he came by the mild, uncomplaining nature for which he was famous:

I first began my career as a puppet operator at the age of eight, when I was encouraged to study under Yoshida Kinshi, who was appearing then at the Horie Theatre. An apprentice's training in those days was very strict in any case, but my teacher was especially severe. When I first became his pupil, it was my task to arrange his footwear at the door and to accompany him when he went out. When he returned home, I was expected to do everything from cleaning the house inside and out to helping in the kitchen. When I finished my other tasks, I used to make dust cloths from old rags. I was obliged to massage the shoulders not only of my teacher but of his wife and daughters as well, supposedly to strengthen my fingers. And my teacher never said to me, "Please massage me," but rather, "You may have the honor now of massaging me." Whenever I went out with him he kept up an uninterrupted stream of complaints, saying I was walking too close or too far away or I wasn't holding the lantern properly. At the theatre it was my job to hold up corpses or tobacco trays at the level of the railing, keeping my hands out of sight (we didn't use a stand in those days). If I moved even the least bit I was immediately scolded. Then, after a while, when I came to practice manipulating the feet, using a puppet suspended from the ceiling, I tried my best to learn, but my teacher would continually hit me with his metal tobacco pipe, saying I was operating the feet clumsily or that I wasn't steady.... At last when I was able to move the feet, I was permitted to appear in the theatre holding a one-man puppet. I spent three full years practicing in this way, but during all this time I didn't receive a penny.... When I got back home at night I never had more than three hours of sleep. I was so sleepy even when I was walking that I would bump into telegraph poles, or fall over mail boxes and doze off on the spot. Many times when I set off for the theatre I felt as if I were about to drop right down into hell. After that kind of training you can see why I became the kind of nincompoop I am today.

Whatever benefit Eiza may have obtained from Yoshida Kinshi's instruction, he never sought guidance from another teacher. He learned entirely by observation of the masters and by helping them with the feet or left hand of their puppets.

Eiza's first appearance at the puppet theatre came when he was twelve. He was assigned a part, considered suitable because of his small stature, which required him to pull a puppet's body and head over his own head, and to climb on the shoulders of another puppeteer. The stunt delighted the audience, especially when it first realized that the feet it could see belonged to a child and not a puppet. At the end of the scene, however, Eiza and the puppet were both dumped unceremoniously into a basket, so painful a jolt that the boy saw stars each time. Eiza assumed the principal operator's part for secondary characters at the age of fifteen, but he still continued to work the feet of the puppets for other operators. One role compelled him to hold a puppet absolutely motionless for twenty minutes. If he so much as budged he was immediately kicked by the principal operator with his high clogs, so viciously that the boy's shins were covered with welts.

Eiza's first important chance came in 1895, when he was twenty-three. A puppeteer who was to have appeared in Dampei's puppet version of the Kabuki play *Kanjinchō* suddenly fell ill, and Eiza was chosen as his substitute. Eiza, who had never before operated a large male puppet, was unprepared for the weight, which proved almost too much for him, but he successfully performed the part.

In the following year Eiza joined the Bunraku Theatre after years of playing in various rival companies. Here too he was entrusted with secondary characters, though on occasion he still operated the feet. But at least Eiza could be reasonably sure that one day he would achieve recognition as a principal operator. Not all puppet operators are so fortunate. There is the famous case of Yoshida Kanshi (1855–1930), the oldest member of the Bunraku company when he died, who was condemned to operate the feet exclusively for forty years. In 1929, the year before his death, various persons from the literary and artistic world presented him with fifty yen—about one month's salary—to console him for his unlucky career. Other men have never gone beyond operating the left hand. Eiza, however, after his first great success in 1907, at the age of thirty-five, quickly established himself as a master. Until his death he and Bungorō divided honors as the chief puppet operators. Both were known for their performances of the female roles, but whereas Bungorō excelled in colorful or even erotic parts, Eiza, probably as a result of his retiring disposition, was better suited to the long-suffering heroines of domestic tragedies.

Whatever role an operator assumes, he must observe its traditions, or if a new work, the traditions of similar parts in older works of the repertory. In addition, he is bound by the traditional appearance of the puppets. A puppet is at once an internal mechanism and an external presence. The operator tries not to let the audience become aware of the various armatures and strings which move the parts of the puppet's body, but he is powerless to change the external features: the head, the wig, the arms and legs, the costuming. A number of possibilities exists in each of these categories, but tradition has long since decided the proper appearance, say, for Matsuōmaru in "The

Village School" scene, and any attempt by the operator to change the accepted view of the role by using an untraditional head or wig would certainly arouse much controversy.

The puppet heads have been divided into different categories. One common division is into good and bad characters, in the following manner:

	Good	Bad
Old man	Kiichi, Masamune, Sadanoshin, Takeuji, Shiratayū	Shūto (father-in-law), Ōjūto Torao
Old woman	Baba (old woman)	Bakuya
Middle-aged man	Kōmei, Bunshichi	Danshichi, Kintoki
Middle-aged woman	Fukeoyama (middle-aged heroine)	Yashio
Young man	Kembishi, Genta, Oniwaka Wakaotoko (young man)	Yokambei, Darasuke
Young woman	Musume (young woman) Shinzō (young courtesan) Keisei (courtesan)	
Clown	Matahei	Onoemon
Female Clown	Ofuku	

In addition to the above heads (some of which are known by variant names) there are heads for children, for various minor comic and eccentric parts, for the supernumerary characters operated by one man, and for the half a dozen or so special roles which have heads used exclusively for them. Some heads have several variations: the Bunshichi head, for example, depending on the role, may or may not be able to open its mouth; the female heads similarly are sometimes able to shut their eyes. The heads are known by the names of characters in famous plays of the past for which the particular heads were originally employed. Kiichi, for example, is the name of an old man in a play first produced in 1731. The same head is used today for such roles as Honzō in *Chūshingura* and Midaroku in "Kumagai's Camp."

In general, each head has a fixed personality, though some shadings exist. Kiichi outwardly shows a stern expression, emphasized by his eyes and eyebrows, but inwardly, we can sense, he possesses deep understanding. This head comes in two sizes, the larger used in the historical plays, and in both gentler and severer expressions, depending on the role. Two shades of coloring are used for Kiichi's face, expressive of slightly different personalities.

The most important head of all is that of Bunshichi, used mainly in the historical plays for middle-aged warriors, impressive figures tormented by a secret grief. Kumagai in "Kumagai's Camp," Matsuōmaru in "The Village School," and Takechi Mitsuhide in *Taikōki*, men of quite different circumstances, are all represented by the Bunshichi head because they share the same essential traits. Shadings in character or in social position are revealed otherwise by the use of appropriate wigs and the costuming, both of which can transform a given head considerably.

The possibility of moving the eyes, eyebrows, and mouth enormously increases the expressive range of the heads, though these movements can be resorted to only infrequently without weakening their effect or else becoming positively comic. For many roles, however, no such range of expression is needed. The young heroes of Chikamatsu's domestic tragedies, for example, exhibit relatively slight changes of mood in the course of a scene, and the heads used for them are accordingly immobile. However, it sometimes happens that different acts of the same play will call for a given character to be portrayed with different heads; thus, Jihei in "The Love Suicides at Amijima" is played with a Genta head in the first act (at the Kawashō Teahouse), but customarily, with a Wakaotoko head in the second act, the scene with his wife at the paper shop. The greatest variety of expression occurs in the villainous or comic parts, the least in the "good" female parts. The Fukeoyama (older woman's) head is equipped with a pin projecting from the lower lip which enables the operator to press the grief-stricken wife's sleeve to her mouth as she restrains her sobs.

The heads are often beautiful examples of carving and deservedly prized as objects of art. The Bunraku company formerly possessed a magnificent collection, many over a century old, but the fire of 1926 and the bombing of 1945 destroyed almost all the best heads. When the company was reorganized in 1946 it was necessary to borrow heads from private collections which had escaped the war. Most of the heads currently employed are recent, carved by a few men working in Tokushima, who also supply the larger puppet heads used in the Tokushima and Awaji theatres. These conscientiously executed heads have proved serviceable in production, but inevitably they lack the artistic excellence of the older examples.

The wigs used in Bunraku are important not only in distinguishing, say, a warrior like Kumagai from a nobleman like Matsuōmaru, but define the age of the characters more precisely than is possible with the head alone. In pre-modern Japan, hairstyles were unmistakably indicative of a person's age and status, and the difference in appearance between a woman of twenty and a woman of twenty-five can still be conveyed quite precisely in a puppet performance by the style of hairdo and the costume even if the head is the same.

Hands and (in the case of the male puppets) feet also vary considerably with the part. Nine commonly used types of hands, and another twenty-four more unusual varieties, have been distinguished. The fingers of the *tsukamite* ("grab hand"), for example, are all independently movable; the *takotsukami* ("octopus grab") permits additionally the movement of the wrist. Needless to say, these hands are appropriate to energetic male puppets, but would not be used for a young lover or for a woman. Most female puppets are equipped with hands which possess independent movement only of the thumbs and wrists; the hands used for old women, however, can exercise movement only of the wrists.

Legs and feet are less complicated; there are six principal varieties for the male puppets, and one each for female and child puppets. They vary depending on whether or not they will be fully visible and also on the size and strength of the character portrayed. Legs and feet are rarely used for the female puppets. In "The Love Suicides at Sonezaki," where it is essential that the heroine's foot be seen, a foot not connected to the puppet's body is pushed out from the puppet's skirts by the third operator at appropriate moments but discarded as soon as it is no longer needed.

In general, Bunraku heads and hands are allowed only the minimum amount of movement necessary. Unless there is some special reason for a character to open his mouth, for example, the head employed for the role will have a fixed mouth; the fewer the moving parts, the more attractive the head or hands. In certain roles, like the courtesan Akoya's in *Dannoura Kabuto Gunki*, the character plays a musical instrument, and specially designed hands are therefore employed. For a few plays also in which a woman in the course of the action reveals her true identity as a demon, a head has been contrived which splits horizontally, revealing a hideous demon's grin. The more grotesque heads, though remarkable examples of the carver's art, are rarely used, and connoisseurs of Bunraku are likely to prefer the Bunshichi or Fukeoyama heads, which symbolize the essence of Bunraku drama.

The operator manipulates not only the puppets but most props figuring in the action. If a sword, lantern or broom must be wielded by a character, the operator inserts his own hand in the puppet's sleeve and holds the object for the puppet, though in a few special instances puppet hands are used which are specially made to hold a brush, fan or drumstick. The props in Bunraku, for the most part identical to those used in Kabuki, are disproportionately large for the puppets. A movable stand is now commonly used to support props not moved much in the course of a scene, though formerly (as Eiza complained) it was customary for an operator to hold the object motionlessly from underneath, often for a quarter of an hour at a time.

The stage settings are designed to reveal immediately the category of play (whether historical or domestic tragedy), the class of society to which the characters belong (nobility, warrior, merchant), or else a particular landscape (riverside, street, forest) which dominates the scene. The conventions of Japanese architecture are invariably followed, but for practical reasons the characters are not required, say, to remove their footwear on entering a house; on the other hand, characters invariably seat themselves when they begin to talk, even if the action occurs in a street without benches or chairs. Such conventions are accepted easily, and any attempt at greater verisimilitude in the settings would only impede the free movements of the operators along the three passages across the stage or on the steps going down from one passage to the next. Occasionally use is made of the *hanamichi*, a raised passageway from the stage to the back of the audience that is an essential feature of Kabuki. In Bunraku the *hanamichi* calls excessive attention to the operators by suddenly exposing all three men to full view, an effect more curious than pleasing.

The presentation of Bunraku plays continues to change as the result of improvements in stage apparatus and shifts in taste. Puppet plays were originally performed out of doors in uniformly bright light, but it is now possible in the theatre to dim or extinguish the illumination, creating new effects. The use of foreign or modern plays has led to the use of new heads with the appropriate features and hairdos, and to trousers, tights, hoopskirts, and other articles of clothing much less successful than kimonos in filling out the rude framework of the Bunraku puppet. An increasing use of devices like the movable stand has made things so much easier for the operators that older members of the company remember nostalgically the difficult demands of the audiences of the past.

Despite such changes in plays and presentation, and a perhaps excessive desire of some members of the Bunraku world to bring the puppet theatre up to date, it remains essentially a traditional art learned, especially the manipulation of the puppets, by the traditional, unscientific methods of transmitting "secrets" from master to disciple over the years. It is a difficult profession to enter, and requires an immense amount of training before the beginner is qualified to appear before the public. No matter how conscientiously he performs when he finally has his chance, the critics are likely to reward his efforts by recalling wistfully the superior artistry of the great men of the past. But each chanter, samisen player, and puppet operator must feel satisfaction when he realizes that his very presence on the Bunraku stage means that he is continuing the traditions of generations of masters before him.

VI. THE GESTURES OF BUNRAKU

EVERY form of stage entertainment performed in keeping with long-standing traditions inevitably develops special, stylized gestures, instantly recognizable to connoisseurs, though not always to persons seeing them for the first time. When, for example, the prince in *Swan Lake* touches his hand to his forehead, the balletomane knows without explanation that the gesture means the young man is straining to catch a glimpse of the swan princess, though a rather similar gesture in a Nō play would signify that the character was weeping. Again, when the Italian operatic tenor places his right hand on his left breast, we may safely assume that he is in love, though the Kabuki actor making a similar gesture might intend us to realize that he is struggling to control overpowering rage. The gestures of the stage, when not directly imitative of universally recognizable phenomena (weeping with sorrow, shuddering with fear, and so on), are derived of course from the habitual gestures of the particular society of which the theatre is a part. The European or Japanese actor shakes his head laterally to signify "no"; the Indian actor makes the same gesture to signify "yes." Both are merely reproducing on the stage the normal daily gestures of their societies. In the puppet theatre, however, the reproduction of believable gestures is complicated by the necessity of reinforcing almost every word with appropriate bodily movements if the wooden figures are not to seem utterly lifeless.

The sculpted puppet faces are deliberately fashioned so that the expression can be markedly altered by moving the eyes, eyebrows or mouth, but these movements are employed relatively seldom, so as not to weaken their effect in the climactic scenes. Changes of expression normally come from the successive poses of the puppet's body. The texts themselves, with their frequent and violent shifts of emotion, favor the almost ceaseless, fluid movements. Without this flow of gestures, indeed, there would be little possibility of dramatic illusion in the puppet theatre.

Gestures performed by actors can be so restrained as to be almost imperceptible at times, yet retain their effect because of the unifying strength of the actor's personality. In the puppet theatre, however, the inability of the puppets to rival the subtlety of movement of a living person has led the operators to choose the opposite extreme: they create an illusion of life by simplifying and intensifying human gestures so as to make the audience feel it is witnessing a distillation of the emotions experienced by the characters on the stage. Nothing, then, can be casual or approximate; a repertory of clearly established gestures is employed to define each moment. Repeated performances of the same work tend to make the gestures almost automatic, and the identification between a puppet and the chief operator may seem unconscious, but a worthy performance requires complete concentration on every gesture. Because gestures form the visual center of the play, the range is far greater than in a theatre of actors, where other means are available.

Two varieties of gesture may be distinguished in Bunraku: the first is a stylized reproduction of familiar human movements, whether the manner of using the body to express grief or joy, or the way a woman sews clothes or plays a musical instrument; the second is not so much a reproduction of human attitudes as an extension of them which permits the operator to display the unique beauty of line that puppets can achieve. The former variety of gestures (known as *furi*) includes as many motions as living people perform; the latter variety (the *kata*) are relatively restricted in number. The creation of a definitive pattern of *furi* and *kata* for a given role is normally a long process, involving constant experimentation by successive operators until experts are agreed that the exact meaning of the text has been visually realized.

The movements of the Bunraku puppets do not constitute a gesture language in the sense, say, that the Kathakali dancers of India can mime every word of a sentence like, "Please come tomorrow at half-past twelve." Not only does the puppet move too slowly in the hands of its three operators for it to depict each word, even when delivered at the pace of the chanter's declamation, but the gestures are intended to underline with broad strokes the central aspect of an utterance rather than to reproduce each word. A choice must be made as to which part of a given phrase will be reinforced by gesture. If, for example, the text reads something like, "I shall be laughed at all over Osaka," the operator may suggest the character's distress at being mocked, or the action of mocking itself, or (with a sweep of the puppet's arm) the vastness of the city, or (if the action is taking place elsewhere) the direction of Osaka.

We cannot be sure of the successive stages undergone by the gestures of the repertory classics before they achieved their present, definitive forms a century or more ago, but we can observe today, especially when new plays are staged (or old plays are revived after a lapse of many years) the process of selection and refinement which probably occurred also in the past. "The Love Suicides at Sonezaki" (*Sonezaki Shinjū*) had not been performed by a Bunraku company for almost 250 years when it was revived in 1955, and no records survived of the *furi* which had originally been employed. The text itself afforded only meagre indications of the gestures intended by the author Chikamatsu Monzaemon. The best clues to the appropriate gestures for the different characters were provided by analogies with similar characters in other works of the repertory. It took considerable time for the operators to settle on the most effective *furi*. Initially, for example, the unhappy lover Tokubei narrated his woes in the first act from a seated position, in keeping with the familiar practice of the puppet theatre, but eventually the operator (Yoshida Tamao) decided that Tokubei's dejection would be more vividly suggested if he stood by a drooping willow as he spoke. Again, the play originally ended as Tokubei, his arm shaking with emotion, held his dagger poised over the throat of the kneeling Ohatsu, but in later performances Tokubei was variously made to drop the dagger in helpless despair, to stab Ohatsu and then himself, or to stab Ohatsu and then turn the point towards himself as the curtain was drawn. Such experimentations continued until the operators felt satisfied that the essential intent of the text had been realized. Nine years after the revival, in 1964, younger operators were given the chance to present their own interpretations of the roles, but they showed themselves disinclined to make innovations; the *furi* for "The Love Suicides at Sonezaki" had already become established. In the case of older works of the repertory, innovation by younger operators would be almost unthinkable.

A great performer who has demonstrated his mastery of the traditional *furi* may, however, choose to depart from tradition on the basis of his individual interpretation of a character. In this way variant traditions of *furi* have been created and preserved by different "family" lines. One well-known example of a variant tradition is found at the outset of the famous monologue from the "Saké Shop" scene in the play *Hadesugata Onna Maiginu*. Hanshichi's wife Osono wonders where her husband, who has run off with another woman, may now be. The great puppeteer Yoshida Bungorō had Osono go to the entrance of the saké shop as if to strain for a glimpse of her husband; she strikes an attitude of anxious reflection, one hand thrust in the bosom of her kimono. The effect of this pose is lovely, but critics objected that it made Osono seem less like a virtuous housewife than a courtesan. In the other tradition of performing the scene, exemplified by Kiritake Monjūrō, Osono pronounces the lines as she absent-mindedly dusts a standing lantern. This *furi*, though visually less charming than Bungorō's, evokes more successfully the character of the devoted wife who, even in the midst of her tormented worries, automatically wipes away the dust she has noticed on the frame of the lamp.

A psychologically true interpretation of each character is the chief goal of the operators, but they seek to embody in the performance not only the meaning of the words of the text but the moments of visual beauty they sense are implicit. This second requirement explains the use of the *kata*, spectacular poses which, unlike the *furi*, may have no direct connection with the text, and may not be necessary even in the general portrayal of a character. A scene without *kata*, even if dramatically effective, lacks something of the peculiar beauty of the art, for it fails to exploit the capacity of puppets to strike ravishing poses which are beyond the physical capacities of a human body. One unusually appealing *kata* is the *ushiroburi*, or "turning to the rear," of female puppets. The effect is to reveal the uninterrupted sweep of the kimono and the lovely undulant lines of the hems as seen from behind. No textual justification is needed for this *kata*, though obviously it fits more easily into certain scenes than others. During the course of Osono's monologue the two varieties of this *kata* are presented. The first (and more spectacular), the *ushiroburi* to the left, begins as Osono moves forward to the sharply accented rhythm of the samisen. She stamps with her right foot, at which point the chief operator, passing the stick for the right arm to the other operator, uses his left hand to move the body counterclockwise until it faces the rear. The other operator, hidden behind the figure, spreads out both sleeves to reveal the full beauty of the costume in an exquisite pose, only presently to touch the sleeves to the face in the gesture of weeping. In the other variety of this *kata*, the *ushiroburi* to the right, the chief operator, instead of entrusting the right arm to the second operator, himself takes the left arm also, and swings the puppet around clockwise to face the rear. This variation does not permit the spreading of the sleeves, but has a quieter, more pathetic quality.

The *kata* for male puppets naturally place great emphasis on the kicking and stamping of the feet with which male puppets are provided. Like the *mie* poses in Kabuki, these *kata* often epitomize by the violent angles of the body the powerful emotions of the character, but unlike the Kabuki *mie*, the Bunraku pose is not static. It consists rather of a series of movements rather like the climax of a dance. The Bunraku and Kabuki *kata* for the same work often differ considerably. In the Kabuki version of the head inspection scene from the "Village School" section of *Sugawara Denju Tenarai Kagami*, for example, the box containing the severed head is placed directly before Matsuōmaru. Then, depending on the variety of *kata* followed by the actor, he may lift the lid with both hands and stare at the head, or he may remove it with one hand, propping up his chin with the other to suggest his physical debility. In Bunraku, the box is placed to Matsuōmaru's right, and the play of gestures between him and the schoolmaster Genzō before the head is actually brought before Matsuōmaru affords a moment of dramatic conflict. Other *kata* for male puppets depend on such properties of the figure as the ability to open the mouth, lift the eyebrows, clench the fists, and so on.

The effect produced on Bunraku audiences by the *kata* for male and female puppets differs considerably, even when the movements themselves are similar. The female *kata*, though lovely to watch, may possess little dramatic significance; the male *kata*, on the other hand, usually occur at climactic moments, and are as appropriate to a particular character as the head or costume.

The movements making up a given *kata* were determined by the puppet operators of the past and are repeated faithfully today as a part of the discipline of the art, in much the way that elements of classical Western ballet are preserved intact, regardless of the work. The more naturalistic *furi* are also governed by long-standing traditions, not only in the basic interpretation of a role but in the details of the gestures. Even the most inconspicuous movements generally obey precedent, for in Bunraku there can be none of the unpremeditated or unconscious actions of people in daily life or of actors on a stage. One master of a century ago wrote a long series of poems (*waka*) offering advice to puppet operators, including:

fumidashi wa	When they start to walk
otoko hidari ni	The man puts forth the left foot,
onna migi;	The woman, the right;
kore inyō no	This is how we distinguish
sabetsu narikeri.	Male and female principles.
odoroki wa	To express surprise
kao shirizokete	You should turn the face away,
ude wo dashi	Put forth the arms,
kobushi wo chū ni	And raise clenched fists in the air
oku mono zo kashi	To achieve the best effect.
warau toki	When they are laughing
otoko wa kata wo	The man must throw his shoulders
souru nari	Into the gesture;
onna wa sode wo	The woman touches her sleeve
atete utsumuku	To her face and gazes down.
yō no naki	The operator
ningyō wa tada	Who does not move in the least
tsuyu hodo ni	A puppet with no
ugokasenu wo ba	Actions required of him
tassha to zo iu.	We call a master artist.

These and the other poems of the series indicate how clearly defined the idiom of the gestures had become. The audiences presumably were no less familiar with such conventions than the operators. But no matter how confining to free expression we may imagine the existence of established *furi* and *kata* to be, in practice there is always a considerable amount of variation from performance to performance. Such differences are due for the most part not to the relatively infrequent instances of an operator deliberately changing an existing pattern, but to the less conspicuous shadings given to the existing pattern by the temperament of the operator. This intrusion of the personality, despite formal patterns, may be found in all the traditional Japanese stage arts. The old saying had it, "Enter the mould, then break it!" by which was meant that a performer who had mastered the traditions could then break them to express his distinctive talents. The great puppet operators execute essentially the same gestures as the mediocre performers, but inevitably there are minute differences which are apparent to the audience and distinguish the true artist from the hack. Even the same man's manipulation of a puppet may vary in response to the atmosphere in the theatre or to a slightly altered tempo from the samisen accompaniment. The established gestures of the puppet theatre do not hamstring the operators and make them mere slaves of tradition; on the contrary, by providing a time-tested basic structure for the performance they enable the superior puppeteer to devote himself to the shadings and colorings of interpretation which are the truly interesting aspect of the art. When we go to hear a celebrated pianist interpret a familiar sonata we do not expect something almost unrecognizably different from previous performances, but rather a fresh attempt to achieve within tradition the ultimate interpretation of the work. With each Bunraku performance too we hope that the combination of tradition and individual talent will make an old masterpiece new again.

PLATES

1. *Yoshitsune Sembonzakura* (1747), by Takeda Izumo and ▷
others, is known especially for the "*Sushi* Shop" scene and the
"Journey" (*michiyuki*). The disinherited Gonta, profiting by
his father's absence from the *sushi* shop, arrives secretly and
calls his mother. (Danshichi head)

2. *Shōutsushi Asagaobanashi* (1832), commonly known as *Asagao Nikki*, contains many popular scenes. Here, Miyuki, separated from her lover Asojirō by a misunderstanding, plays a *koto* at a country inn to earn her living. She has gone blind from weeping over her griefs, as the closed eyes of the puppet head show. (Musume head)

3. "The Village School" scene from *Sugawara Denju Tenarai Kagami* ▷ (1746), by Takeda Izumo and others, is a great popular favorite. The evil Prime Minister, learning that the son of his hated rival is attending a village school, sends the nobleman Matsuōmaru to take the boy's head. Matsuōmaru, having identified the head of his own son as the one he had been commanded to take, rises to his feet and says he will resign from the Prime Minister's service. (Bunshichi head)

◁ 4. *Ehon Taikōki* (1799), by Chikamatsu Yanagi and others, describes the warfare of the sixteenth century. Jūjirō, the only son of the warrior Mitsuhide, staggers home badly wounded from the battlefield. Leaning on his sword, he describes the defeat. (Genta head)

5. *Chūshingura* (1748), by Takeda Izumo and others, is perhaps the greatest play of the puppet theatre. In the third of the eleven acts Enya Hangan, taunted by the evil Kō no Moronao because he failed to offer the expected bribe, finally draws his sword and slashes at Moronao. (Moronao: Ōjūto head)

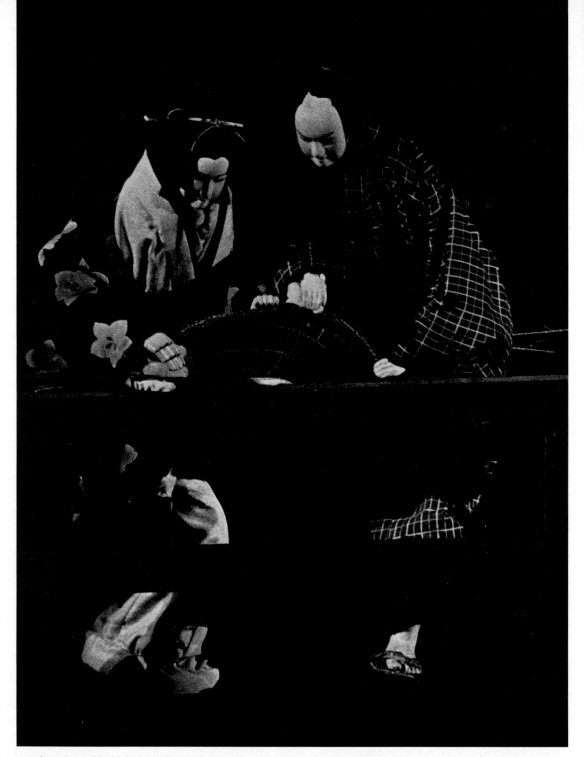

6 and 7. *Sonezaki Shinjū* (or "The Love Suicides at Sonezaki") was written by Chikamatsu Monzaemon in 1703. In the final scene, Tokubei and his sweetheart Ohatsu, a courtesan, journey to their death. (Tokubei: Genta head; Ohatsu: Keisei head)

(6) They pause a moment on a bridge and look down at the river.

(7) When they have reached the wood of Sonezaki, Tokubei holds his dagger poised over Ohatsu's throat. She urges him to kill her quickly.

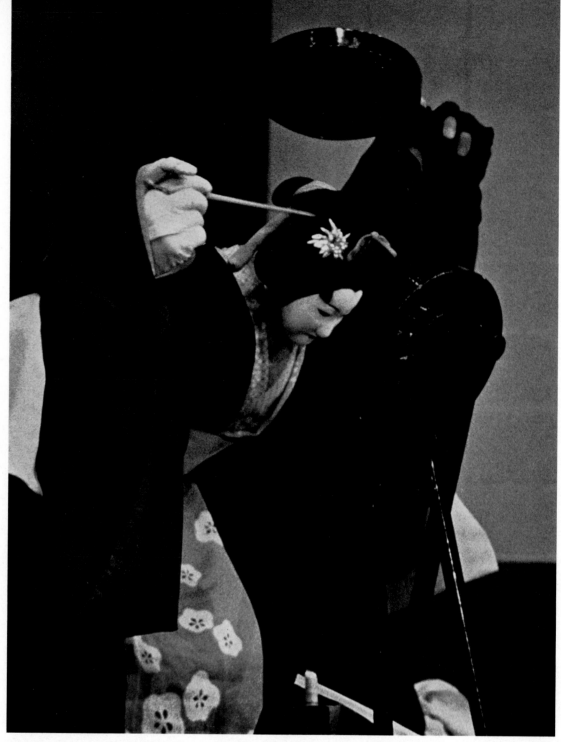

8. *Shimpan Utazaimon* (1780), by Chikamatsu Hanji, is frequently called "Osome and Hisamatsu" after the ill-fated lovers. The scene at Nozaki Village begins as Omitsu, a country girl who is Osome's rival for Hisamatsu's love, touches up her hair at word that he is on his way. (Musume head)

9. *Hadesugata Onna Maiginu* (1773), by Takemoto Saburo- ▷ bei and others, has a famous scene at the saké shop of Han-shichi, a young man who has deserted his wife Osono for the prostitute Sankatsu. Here, Sankatsu, carrying her small daughter, arrives at the shop entrance. (Keisei head)

10. Fukeoyama ("mature woman") head
This head is used for women of intelligence, passionately devoted to
their children, and loyal to their husbands. Only the eyes move, but
a needle is provided at the side of the mouth to catch the sleeve or
hand towel in a gesture of weeping.

11. Ōdanshichi ("large Danshichi") head
First used for Watōnai in "The Battles of Coxinga" (1715), ▷
it represents warriors of violent temperament. The eyebrows
and mouth move; the eyes move laterally.

12. The operator pulls one or more strings to make the eyes cross or (13) to lower the head and the eyebrows, or (14) to open the mouth in a shout of command.

15. The attention of the spectators is at times drawn from the stage to the chanter seated on a dais to their right, for the pleasure of seeing the range of expressions that cross his face. The samisen player seldom attracts attention to himself, though occasional virtuoso passages may make the audience applaud.

16. The operation of a three-man puppet, as seen from the wings, appears so unwieldy that it is hard to believe a dramatic illusion could be achieved. The chief operator, standing on high *geta*, holds the puppet above the floor level indicated by the top of the partition; the other two operators, less conspicuous because hooded and shod in low *zōri*, follow his leads almost instinctively.

17. Behind the scenes at the puppet theatre of Yamamoto Tosa-no-jō, about 1690. To the left, concealed from the public by a curtain, the operators hold puppets above the railing. The chanter and samisen player, also out of the audience's sight, sit on a dais. Puppets not in use dangle from above. Each puppet was operated by one man.

18. Entrance of Temma Hachidayū's theatre in Edo, about 1685. A customer is paying the admission fee to the man seated on the platform. The man in black is the door manager. The entrance itself (under the sign) was made extremely small in order to prevent persons who had not paid from sneaking inside.

76

19. A group of Edo chanters of the 1690s during rehearsal. They beat time with their fans.

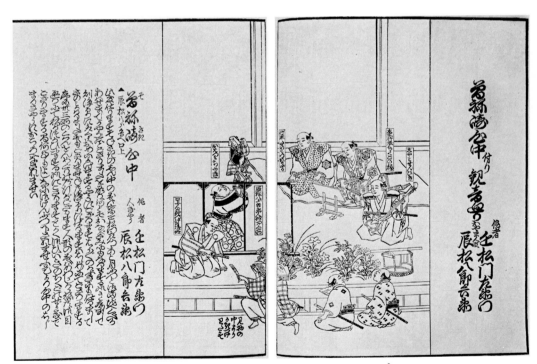

20. This stylized drawing of a performance of "The Love Suicides at Sonezaki" (1703) depicts the *michiyuki* scene. Tatsumatsu Hachirobei operates the puppet for Ohatsu in view of the audience; at the same time, the chanter Gidayū and his assistants are visible to the right. The curtain speech delivered by Tatsumatsu at the first performance (left) explains how Chikamatsu came to write the play.

21. An illustration of Chikamatsu's play "The Mirror of Craftsmen of the Emperor Yōmei" (1705), showing in stylized form the puppet operator Tatsumatsu Hachirobei and the chanter Takemoto Gidayū performing in full view of the audience.

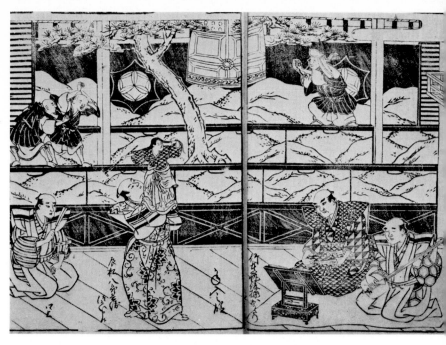

22. A performance in 1765 of *Ranjatai Nitta Keizu* by Chikamatsu Hanji, showing three-man puppets of the variety still used. The chanter and samisen player sit behind a bamboo blind stripped to the waist, no doubt because this performance took place in summer.

LIST OF PLAYS

Akoya no Kotozeme: See *Dannoura Kabuto Gunki.*

Amida no Munewari (阿弥陀胸割). Sixteenth century play by unknown author, no longer performed.

Asagao Nikki: See *Shō Utsushi Asagaobanashi.*

Ashiya Dōman Ōuchi Kagami (芦屋道満大内鑑) by Takeda Izumo. Five acts, of which the fourth (*Yasuna-uchi*) is most frequently performed. 1734.

Ataka no Seki (安宅関). Music by Toyozawa Dampei. A dance play adapted from the Kabuki work *Kanjin-chō.* 1895.

Benkei Jōshi: See *Goshozakura Horikawa Youchi.*

Chest-Splitting of Amida: See *Amida no Munewari.*

Chikagoro Kawara no Tatehiki (近頃河原の達引) by Tamekawa Sōsuke, Tsutsui Hanji, and Nagawa Shimesuke. Three acts, of which the second (*Horikawa*) is frequently performed. 1785.

Chūshingura: See *Kanadehon Chūshingura.*

Daidairi Ōtomo no Matori (大内裏大友真鳥) by Takeda Izumo. Five acts. The play is not commonly performed at present. 1725.

Dango-uri: See *Ne mo Sayuru Haru no Usuzuki.*

Dannoura Kabuto Gunki (壇浦兜軍記) by Matsuda Bunkōdō and Hasegawa Senshi. Five acts, of which the third (*Akoya no Kotozeme*) is frequently performed. 1732.

Danshichi Kurobei: See *Natsumatsuri Naniwa Kagami.*

Date Kurabe Okuni Kabuki (伊達競阿国戯場) by Tatsuta Benji, Yoshida Kigan, and Utei Emba. Ten acts. 1779.

Date Sōdō: See *Date Kurabe Okuni Kabuki.*

Dōjōji: See *Kyōganoko Musume Dōjōji.*

Domomata: See *Keisei Hangokō.*

Ehon Taikōki (絵本太功記) by Chikamatsu Yanagi, Chikamatsu Kosuiken, and Chikamatsu Senyōken. Thirteen acts, of which the first (*Nijōjō Haizen*), second (*Honnōji*), sixth (*Myōshinji*), and tenth (*Amagasaki*) are still frequently performed. 1799.

En no Gyōja Ōminezakura (役行者大峰桜) by Takeda Geki, Yoshida Kanshi, and Miyoshi Shōraku. Five acts. 1751.

Futatsu Chōchō Kuruwa Nikki (双蝶々曲輪日記) by Takeda Izumo, Miyoshi Shōraku, and Namiki Sōsuke. Nine acts of which the second (*Sumō-mae*), sixth (*Hashimoto*), seventh (*Kyōran*), and eighth (*Hiki-mado*) are frequently performed. 1749.

Gappō's Daughter Tsuji: See *Sesshū Gappō ga Tsuji*

Go Taiheiki Shiraishibanashi (碁太平記白石噺) by Kino Jōtarō, Utei Emba, and Yō Yōtai. Eleven acts, of which the seventh (*Yoshiwara Ageya*) is frequently performed. 1780.

Goshozakura Horikawa Youchi (御所桜堀川夜討) by Matsuda Bunkōdō and Miyoshi Shōraku. Five acts, of which the third (*Benkei Jōshi*) and fourth (*Tōyata Monogatari*) are most frequently performed. 1737.

Hadesugata Onna Maiginu (艶容女舞衣) by Takemoto Saburobei, Toyotake Ōritsu, and Yatami Hei-shichi. Three acts, of which the third (*Sakaya*) is frequently performed. 1772.

Hamlet adapted by Ōnishi Toshio. 1956.

Heike Nyogo no Shima (平家女護島) by Chikamatsu Monzaemon. Five acts, of which the second (*Kikai-ga-shima*) is most frequently performed. 1719.

Hidakagawa Iriaizakura (日高川入相花王) by Takeda Koizumo, Chikamatsu Hanji, Takemoto Saburobei, Kitamado Goichi, and Nibudō. Five acts, of which the fourth (*Hidakagawa*) is most frequently performed. 1759.

Hiragana Seisuiki (ひらがな盛衰記) by Miyoshi Shōraku, Matsuda Bunkōdō, Asada Kakei, Takeda Koizumo, and Takeda Izumo. Five acts, of which the second (*Genta Kandō*), third (*Sakaro*), and fourth (*Kan-zaki Ageya*) are frequently performed. 1739.

Honchō Nijūshi Kō (本朝廿四孝) by Chikamatsu Hanji, Miyoshi Shōraku, Takeda Inaba, Takeda Hei-shichi, Takeda Koide, and Takemoto Saburobei. Five acts, of which the third (*Kansuke Sumika*) and fourth (*Jusshu Kō* and *Kitsunebi*) are frequently performed. 1766.

Ichinotani Futaba Gunki (一谷嫩軍記) by Namiki Sōsuke, Namiki Shōzō, Asada Itchō, Namioka Geiji, Naniwa Sanzō, and Toyotake Jinroku. Five acts, of which the third (*Kumagai Jinya*) is still frequently performed. 1731.

Igagoe Dōchū Sugoroku (伊賀越道中双六) by Chikamatsu Hanji and Chikamatsu Kasaku. Ten acts, of which the sixth (*Numazu*), and eighth (*Okazaki*) are frequently performed. 1783.

Imoseyama Onna Teikin (妹背山婦女庭訓) by Chikamatsu Hanji, Matsuda Baku, Sakai Zempei, Miyoshi Shōraku, and Chikamatsu Tōnan. Five acts, of which all but the fifth are frequently performed. 1771.

Ise Ondo Koi no Netaba (伊勢音頭恋寝刃) original Kabuki play by Chikamatsu Tokusō (1796). Four acts, of which the third (*Aburaya*) is the only one performed. 1838.

Kagamiyama Kokyō no Nishikie (加賀見山旧錦絵) by Yō Yōtai. Eleven acts, of which only the sixth (*Zōri-uchi*) and seventh (*Nagatsubone* and *Okuniwa* scenes) are performed at present. 1782.

Kagekiyo Victorious: See *Shusse Kagekiyo*.

Kamakura Sandaiki (鎌倉三代記) probably by Chika-matsu Hanji. Nine acts, of which the seventh (*Kinugawa Mura*) is most frequently performed. 1770.

Kanadehon Chūshingura (仮名手本忠臣蔵) by Takeda Izumo, Miyoshi Shōraku, and Namiki Sōsuke. Eleven acts, all commonly performed. 1748.

Kasaneizutsu: See *Shinjū Kasaneizutsu*.

Keisei Hangokō (傾城反魂香) by Chikamatsu Monzae-mon. Three acts, of which the first (*Tosa Shōgen Kankyo*) is most frequently performed. 1708.

Kiichi Hōgen Sanryaku no Maki (鬼一法眼三略巻) by Matsuda Bunkōdō and Hasegawa Senshi. Five acts, of which the third (*Kikubatake*) and fifth (*Gojō Ōhashi*) only are at present performed. 1731.

Kikubatake: See *Kiichi Hōgen Sanryaku no Maki*.

Kishihime: See below.

Kishi no Himematsu Kutsuwa Kagami (岸姫松轡鑑) by Toyotake Ōritsu, Wakatake Fuemi, Fukumatsu Tōsuke, and Namiki Eisuke. Five acts, of which the third (*Asahina Jōshi*) is most frequently performed. 1762.

Koharu Jihei: See *Shinjū Ten no Amijima*.

Koi no Tayori Yamato Ōrai (恋飛脚大和往来) by Suga Sensuke and Wakatake Fuemi. Two acts. An adaptation of *Meido no Hikyaku*. 1773.

Koinyōbō Somewake Tazuna (恋女房染分手綱) by Yoshida Kanshi and Miyoshi Shōraku. Thirteen acts, of which the tenth (*Dōchū Sugoroku* and *Shigenoi Kowakare* scenes) is frequently performed. 1751.

Kokaji (小鍛治) by Kimura Tomiko. A dance play adapted from the Nō drama of the same title. 1941.

Kumagai's Camp: See *Ichinotani Futaba Gunki*.

Kuzunoha: See *Ashiya Dōman Ōuchi Kagami*.

Kyōganoko Musume Dōjōji (京鹿子娘道成寺). Author unknown. A dance play. 1810.

Love Suicides at Amijima: See *Shinjū Ten no Amijima*
Love Suicides at Sonezaki: See *Sonezaki Shinjū*.

Madame Butterfly, adapted by Ōnishi Toshio. 1956.

Meiboku Sendai Hagi (伽羅先代萩) by Matsu Kanshi, Takahashi Buhei, and Yoshida Kakumaru. Nine acts, of which the sixth (*Goten* and *Yukashita*) is frequently performed. 1785.

Meido no Hikyaku (冥途の飛脚) by Chikamatsu Mon-zaemon. Three acts, all of which are commonly performed. 1711.

Mekura Kagekiyo: See *Musume Kagekiyo Yashima Nikki*.

Miracle at Tsubosaka Temple: See *Tsubosaka Reigenki*.

Mirror of Craftsmen of the Emperor Yōmei: See *Yōmei Tennō Shokunin Kagami*.

Modoribashi (戻橋). Author unknown. A dance play adapted from the "Modoribashi" scene in *Ōeyama Shutendōji*. Date of first performance not clear.

Mōjōzakura Yuki no Miyashiro (盲杖桜雪社). Author unknown. A dance play. 1884.

Moritsuna's Camp: See *Ōmi Genji Senjin Yakata*.

Musume Kagekiyo Yashima Nikki (嬢景清八島日記) by Wakatake Fuemi, Koku Zōsu, and Nakamura

Akei. Five acts, of which the third (*Hyūgashima*) is most frequently performed. 1764.

Natsumatsuri Naniwa Kagami (夏祭浪花鑑) by Namiki Sōsuke, Miyoshi Shōraku, and Takeda Koizumo. Nine acts, of which the third (*Sumiyoshi Hambe*), sixth (*Sabu-uchi*), and seventh (*Nagamachi Ura*) are frequently performed. 1745.

Nebiki no Kadomatsu (寿の門松) by Chikamatsu Mon-zaemon. Three acts. A revised version entitled *Futatsu Chōchō Kuruwa Nikki* is usually performed. 1718.

Ne mo Sayuru Haru no Usuzuki (音冴春臼月). Author unknown. A dance play. 1915.

Nigatsudō Rōben Sugi no Yurai (二月堂良弁杉由来). Author unknown. One act, four scenes, of which the last two scenes (*Tōdaiji* and *Nigatsudō*) are fre-quently performed. 1887.

Nijūshi Kō: See *Honchō Nijūshi Kō*.

Ōeyama Shutendōji (大江山酒呑童子). Author unknown. Sixteen acts. 1854.

Ohatsu Tokubei: See *Sonezaki Shinjū*.

Ōmi Genji Senjin Yakata (近江源氏先陣館) by Chika-matsu Hanji, Miyoshi Shōraku, Yatami Heishichi, etc. Nine acts, of which the eighth (*Moritsuna Jinya*) is most frequently performed. 1769.

Ōshū Adachi ga Hara (奥州安達原) by Takeda Izumo, Chikamatsu Hanji, Takemoto Saburobei, and Kitamado Goichi. Five acts, of which the third (*Sodehagi Saimon*) is frequently performed. 1762.

Oshun Dembei: See *Chikagoro Kawara no Tatehiki*.

Osome Hisamatsu: See *Shimpan Utazaimon*.

Osono's Monologue: See *Hadesugata Onna Maiginu*.

Otokodate Itsutsu Karigane (男作五雁金) by Takeda Izumo. Seven acts. This play is not performed at present. 1742.

Ranjatai Nitta Keizu (蘭奢待新田系図) by Chikamatsu Hanji, Takeda Heishichi, and Takemoto Saburobei. This play is not performed at present. 1765.

Rōben Sugi: See *Nigatsudō Rōben Sugi no Yurai*.

Sakaya: See *Hadesugata Onna Maiginu*.

Sannin Zatō: See *Mōjōzakura Yuki no Miyashiro*.

Sanyūshi Homare no Nikudan (三勇士名誉肉弾) by Matsui Shōō. Not currently performed. 1932.

Sembonzakura: See *Yoshitsune Sembonzakura*.

Sendai Hagi: See *Meiboku Sendai Hagi*.

Sesshū Gappō ga Tsuji (摂州合邦辻) by Suga Sensuke and Wakatake Fuemi. Two acts, of which the second (*Gappō-uchi*) is frequently performed. 1773.

Shigenoi Kowakare: See *Koi Nyōbō Somewake Tazuna*.

Shimpan Utazaimon (新版歌祭文) by Chikamatsu Hanji. Two acts, the first (*Nozakimura*) and second (*Aburaya*) are commonly performed. 1780.

Shinjū Kasaneizutsu (心中重井筒) by Chikamatsu Mon-zaemon. Three acts, of which the first (*Konya*) and second (*Rokken-chō*) are presently performed. 1707.

Shinjū Ten no Amijima (心中天網島) by Chikamatsu Monzaemon. Three acts, all commonly performed. 1720.

Shin Usuyuki Monogatari (新薄雪物語) by Matsuda Bunkōdō, Miyoshi Shōraku, Ogawa Hampei, and Takeda Koizumo. Three acts. This play is not commonly performed. 1741.

Shiraishibanashi: See *Go Taiheiki Shiraishibanashi*.

Shokatsu Kōmei Kanae Gundan (諸葛孔明鼎軍談) by

Takeda Izumo. Five acts. This play is not performed at present. 1724.

Shō Utsushi Asagaobanashi (生写朝顔話) by Yamada Kakashi. Five acts, of which the first *(Ujigawa Hotarugari)* and fourth *(Shimada Yadoya* and *Ōigawa)* are frequently performed. 1832.

Shunkan: See *Heike Nyogo no Shima.*

Shusse Kagekiyo (出世景清) by Chikamatsu Monzaemon. Five acts. This play is at present not performed. 1686.

Soga Heir: See *Yotsugi Soga.*

Sonezaki Shinjū (曾根崎心中) by Chikamatsu Monzaemon. One act, three scenes, all commonly performed. 1703.

Sugawara Denju Tenarai Kagami (菅原伝授手習鑑) by Takeda Izumo, Miyoshi Shōraku, Namiki Sōsuke, and Takeda Koizumo. Five acts, all frequently performed. 1746.

Summer Festival: See *Natsumatsuri Naniwa Kagami.*

Taijū: See *Ehon Taikōki.*

Taikōki: See *Ehon Taikōki.*

Tamamonomae Asahi no Tamoto (玉藻前曦袂) by Chikamatsu Baishiken and Sagawa Tōta. Five acts, of which the third *(Dōshun Yakata)* is most frequently performed. 1806.

Tamba Yosaku Matsuyo no Komurobushi (丹波与作待夜の小室節) by Chikamatsu Monzaemon. Three acts. A revision entitled *Koi Nyōbō Somewake Tazuna* is more frequently performed than this original. 1708.

Terakoya: See *Sugawara Denju Tenarai Kagami.*

Three Heroes, Glorious Human Bullets: See *Sanyūshi Homare no Nikudan.*

Tōkaidōchū Hizakurige (東海道中膝栗毛). Original story by Jippensha Ikku. 1919.

Tōkaidō Yotsuya Kaidan (東海道四谷怪談) by Tsuruya Namboku (originally a Kabuki play). Five acts. 1825.

Tsubosaka Reigenki (壺坂霊験記) adapted by Toyozawa Dampei and his wife Chika from an earlier work. One act. 1879.

Tsuri Onna (釣女) composed by Tsurusawa Dōhachi. A dance play adapted from a *kyōgen* bearing the same title. 1938.

Umegawa Chūbei: See *Meido no Hikyaku.*

Village School: See *Sugawara Denju Tenarai Kagami.*

Yōmei Tennō Shokunin Kagami (用明天皇職人鑑) by Chikamatsu Monzaemon. Five acts. This play is at present not performed. 1705.

Yoshitsune Sembonzakura (義経千本桜) by Takeda Izumo, Miyoshi Shōraku, and Namiki Sōsuke. Five acts, of which the second *(Tokaiya),* third *(Konomi* and *Sushiya* scenes), and fourth *(Michiyuki, Yoshino,* and *Kawatsura Yakata* scenes) are frequently performed. 1747.

Yotsugi Soga (世継曾我) by Chikamatsu Monzaemon. Five acts. No longer performed. 1683.

Yotsuya Kaidan: See *Tōkaidō Yotsuya Kaidan.*

Yūgiri Awa no Naruto (夕霧阿波鳴門) by Chikamatsu Monzaemon. Three acts, of which the first *(Yoshidaya)* is frequently performed. 1712.

SHORT BIBLIOGRAPHY

Bowers, Faubion. *Japanese Theatre*. New York: Hill and Wang, 1960. Mainly devoted to Kabuki, but contains also a general introduction to Bunraku and the translation of a scene from *Sesshū Gappō ga Tsuji* ("Gappo and his Daughter Tsuji.")

Chikaishi Yasuaki (近石泰秋). *Jōruri Meisaku Shū* (浄瑠璃名作集). Tokyo: Kodansha, 1950. Two vols. Scenes from the most celebrated *jōruri* plays, annotated with special attention given to performance on the Bunraku stage.

Engeki Hakubutsukan (演劇博物館), (ed.). *Engeki Hyakka Daijiten* (演劇百科大事典). Tokyo: Heibonsha, 1960-62. A six-vol. dictionary of the theatre; invaluable for the study of Bunraku.

Engeki Hakubutsukan (演劇博物館), (ed.). *Geinō Jiten* (芸能辞典). Tokyo: Tōkyōdō, 1953. A useful one-volume dictionary of the arts which includes articles on various aspects of Bunraku.

Inoue, Jukichi. *Chushingura or Forty-Seven Ronin*. Tokyo: Maruzen, 1937 (4th edition). A complete translation of the celebrated play.

Kawatake Shigetoshi (河竹繁俊). *Nihon Engeki Zenshi* (日本演劇全史). Tokyo: Iwanami Shoten, 1959. An exceptionally detailed general history of the Japanese theatre which includes much material on Bunraku.

Keene, Donald. *The Battles of Coxinga*. London: Taylor's Foreign Press, 1951. A complete translation of Chikamatsu's play *Kokusenya Kassen* (國性爺合戦), together with an introduction treating the history of *jōruri* and the background of the play.

Keene, Donald. *Major Plays of Chikamatsu*. New York: Columbia University Press, 1961. Complete translations of eleven plays, together with an introduction.

Kiritake Monjūrō (桐竹紋十郎) and Tsurusawa Seijirō (鶴澤清二郎). *Bunraku no Ningyō to Samisen*. Nagoya: Bunraku Kenkyūkai, 1944. Random recollections by a leading puppet operator and samisen player, valuable for personal glimpses of Bunraku, as seen from the inside.

Malm, William. *Japanese Music and Musical Instruments*. Tokyo: Tuttle, 1959. The best book in a Western language on the subject.

Miyao Shigeo (宮尾しげを). *Bunraku Ningyō Zufu* (文楽人形図譜). Tokyo: Jidaisha, 1942. An enchanting study of the Bunraku puppets, with drawings of every variety of head, hand, leg, prop, etc. Filled with odd bits of information which only a person deeply familiar with Bunraku could possess.

Miyake Shūtarō (三宅周太郎). *(Shimpen) Bunraku no Kenkyū* (新編文楽の研究). Tokyo: Sōgensha, 1947. Essays on performers and performances. Interesting especially for its picture of Bunraku immediately after the end of the war in 1945.

Mori Shū (森修). *Chikamatsu Monzaemon* (近松門左衛門). Kyoto: Sanichi Shobō, 1959. An excellent account of the career and artistry of Chikamatsu.

Oda Sakunosuke (織田作之助). *Bunraku no Hito* (文楽の人). Tokyo: Hakuōsha, 1946. An absorbingly written account of the career of the first Yoshida Eiza, together with a shorter essay on Yoshida Bungorō.

Ōnishi Shigetaka (大西重孝) and Yoshinaga Takao (吉永孝雄). *Bunraku*. Tokyo: Kōdansha, 1959. A large collection of Bunraku photographs, together with excellent short essays by various authorities on different aspects of the art.

Ozawa Yoshikuni (小澤愛圀). *Daitōa Kyōeiken no Ningyō-geki* (大東亜共榮圏の人形劇). Tokyo: Mita Bungaku Shuppambu, 1944. Despite the ultranationalistic title, this is a scholarly study of the puppet theatre in various parts of Asia.

Saitō Seijirō (齊藤清二郎). *Bunraku Kashira no Kenkyū* (文楽首の研究). Tokyo: Aterie Sha, 1943. A well-illustrated study of puppet heads by an authority.

Scott, A. C. *The Puppet Theatre of Japan*. Tokyo: Tuttle, 1963. A general introduction.

Shively, Donald H. *The Love Suicides at Amijima*. Cambridge: Harvard University Press, 1953. Complete translation of Chikamatsu's great play, together with an introduction.

Takemoto Tsunadayū (竹本綱太夫). *Denden Mushi* (でんでん虫). Osaka: Nunoi Shobō, 1964. An amusingly written autobiography and book of reminiscences by a gifted chanter.

Tanabe Hisao (田辺尚雄). *Samisen Ongaku Shi* (三味線音楽史). Tokyo: Sōshisha, 1963. The history of the samisen, its development, and its music. The author is a noted scholar of Japanese music.

Tsunoda Ichirō (角田一郎). *Ningyōgeki no Seiritsu ni kansuru Kenkyū* (人形劇の成立に関する研究). Osaka: Asahiya Shoten, 1963. A massive study of the puppet theatre in Japan up to the middle of the 17th century. The best work on the subject.

Utsumi Shigetarō (内海繁太郎). *Ningyō Jōruri to Bunraku* (人形浄瑠璃と文楽). Tokyo: Hakusuisha, 1958. An uninterestingly assembled collection of facts about Bunraku.

Utsumi Shigetarō. *Ningyō Shibai to Chikamatsu no Jōruri* (人形芝居と近松の浄瑠璃). Tokyo: Hakusuisha, 1940. A compendium of material relating to the puppet theatre in Chikamatsu's day and earlier.

Wakatsuki Yasuji (若月保治). *Ningyō Jōruri Shi Kenkyū* (人形浄瑠璃史研究). Tokyo: Sakurai Shoten, 1943. An excellent history of the *jōruri*.

Watsuji Tetsurō (和辻哲郎). *Nihon Geijutsu Shi Kenkyū* (日本藝術史研究). Tokyo: Iwanami Shoten, 1955. An important examination of materials available for study of Bunraku and Kabuki in their early periods.

Yokoyama Tadashi (横山正). *Jōruri Ayatsuri Shibai no Kenkyū* (浄瑠璃操芝居の研究). Tokyo: Kazama Shobō, 1963. A splendid study of the texts and literary qualities of plays by Chikamatsu and later dramatists.

Yoshida Bungorō (吉田文五郎). *Bungorō Geidan* (文五郎芸談). Tokyo: Sakurai Shoten, 1947. Recollections and opinions by the great puppet operator.

INDEX

LEARNING RESOURCES

CENTER

East Peoria, Illinois